PENGUIN VEER

NAGROTA UNDER SIEGE

Bhaavna Arora is the bestselling author of four books, a teacher, an educationist and a corporate trainer. Bhaavna dons many hats, but at the core of it, she is deeply devoted to the Indian Armed Forces, and equally passionate about penning down their true stories and life experiences. She is an Indian who is in awe of the bravery and courage shown by the Indian Army in dire times.

Writing is akin to breathing for her, and she embraces life afresh with every story. Her works reflect the intensity, depth of research and involvement she pours into every word.

In writing this book, she has travelled back in time with those who have lost their dear ones, feeling their pain and loss. For Bhaavna, that loss is personal in many ways, as the brave hearts died protecting us. This book is an honest attempt to glorify and celebrate the bravery of our soldiers.

'Real-life stories of bravery and sacrifice have always motivated me and this book, *Nagrota Under Siege*, details a deadly fidayeen attack and how it was countered. The strength of the Indian Army and the work they do in order to keep us safe is well known. This book brings alive many real-life soldier heroes and the women they love, who were caught up in a terror attack that could have become a terrible hostage crisis but for our brave hearts doing all they did. I recommend you read it to feel it'—**Anupam Kher, actor, director and producer, Padma Shri, Padma Bhushan**

'Too little has been said about the valour of those who defended the Nagrota base in 2016. Bhaavna's searing, heartfelt account should give the brave families of Akshay, Kunal and Chittaranjan the beginnings of closure in a story the country sadly missed. It was thanks to the indomitable Meghna Girish and the other two families that a semblance of memory remains aflame. This book immortalizes them and provides telling clues about why India owes answers to every man or woman lost'—**Shiv Aroor, journalist and bestselling author**

'Bhaavna, like all times, has surprised me with this one. On reading this masterpiece, it feels as if she was there when all this was happening. Impeccable narration and in-depth research are the hallmarks of this book'—**Major Gaurav Arya (retd), editor-in-chief, Chanakya Forum**

'Turning the pages of *Nagrota Under Siege* is like reporting on the horrors of the Nagrota terror strike all over again. A must-read'—**Gaurav C. Sawant, managing editor and anchor, India Today TV and Aaj Tak**

'On 29 November 2016, the Nagrota garrison near Jammu was struck by a harrowing terrorist attack. In her riveting account, Bhaavna pulls readers into the heart of this dark day, bringing to life the intense drama and heroism that unfolded. What sets this book apart is its profound exploration of the soldiers' personal lives. Bhaavna goes beyond the battlefield to present these men not just as warriors but as fathers, husbands and sons. Her poignant depiction of their lives and the impact of their loss serve as a powerful reminder of the human cost of conflict and the enduring spirit of those who serve. This gripping narrative not only chronicles a moment of extraordinary valour but also humanizes the soldiers behind the uniforms, offering readers a deeply moving tribute to their sacrifice and resilience'—**Lieutenant General Deependra Singh Hooda, PVSM, UYSM, AVSM, VSM and Bar, ADC (retd), former general officer commanding-in-chief, Northern Command, Indian Army**

'Bhaavna Arora's stories and books showcase immense research and the deep human side of her characters and suspense, all woven with some very realistically constructed combat scenes when she writes about the Indian Army. These stories also reflect her own pedigree—a fourth-generation army brat—and her love for the army and the nation. After her last extraordinary life story about the Kashmiri army officer Lt Ummer Fayaz, who was brutally murdered by militants while attending a family wedding, she has authored yet another extraordinary book, *Nagrota Under Siege*. It is a pity that in less than eight years, our public at large has forgotten about the Nagrota incident, its valorous operation and the sacrifice of seven brave hearts. That happens because, as she writes, 'What good is a sacrifice if not chronicled?' *Nagrota Under Siege* is a compelling, goosebumpy read, which should make this extraordinary story live through all times to come'—**Gen. V.P. Malik (retd), former chief of the army staff during the Kargil War**

'*Nagrota Under Siege* is a gripping retelling of a dastardly attack on one of our cantonments in the north-western sectors by well-trained jihadis from across the border. It is one of the most well-researched pieces of writing that I have come across. The author deserves our appreciation both for her painstaking research and her unique writing style. The book reads like a taut screenplay where disparate characters are introduced to us one by one independently, and come together only on the day of reckoning in a hair-raising encounter where brave hearts from our army are locked in battle with the infiltrators. The author has done a great service to our armed forces by documenting an unfortunate event that should never have happened, where our brave officers make the supreme sacrifice fighting for their country. An unmissable and unputdownable book that I would strongly recommend to one and all'—**Neeraj Kumar, former commissioner of police, Delhi; former DGP, Goa; former DGP (Prisons), Delhi; former head, Anti-Corruption and Security Unit, Board of Control for Cricket in India; and former joint director, CBI**

'A prolific writer and storyteller, Bhaavna Arora has the knack of weaving her stories in such a way that you get transported to the environment she draws you into and remain transfixed till the very end. Her stories are well researched and detailed, giving glimpses of life in the army. Her ability to humanize each soldier and their family members in her stories touches a chord with anyone who reads her books. In *Nagrota Under Siege*, Bhaavna has beautifully stitched stories of the warriors and their family members, delving into their personal lives in simple, lucid and free-flowing language, so that anyone who reads the book can easily absorb the essence of army life and will relate to the individuals being described. My compliments and good wishes to Bhaavna Arora for bringing out this inspiring book, as also for her stupendous hard work in painstakingly collecting all the factual data and joining the dots. Her ability and brilliance in bringing out these stories exemplify her commitment to people in uniform and recognize her as being the daughter of an army officer. In her own way, she is paying homage to each of these valiant soldiers and their family members. Kudos to her for that'—**Lieutenant General Pattacheruvanda Chengappa Thimayya, PVSM, VSM (retd), twenty first general officer commanding-in-chief, Army Training Command**

'*Nagrota Under Siege* is a hallmark of good writing. It's rare when an in-depth knowledge of military tactics, weaponry, terrorism and the angst of being a soldier's wife and family member is brought together in an authentic presentation. The book is a saga of discipline, brotherhood and patriotism. It is also a story of the coming together of military and civilian agencies directed towards the same goal—payback for a dastardly deed. Combining investigation and literature into a brisk yet emotional read, Bhaavna Arora grabs you by the windpipe and doesn't let go until you experience the soul-shattering conclusion. Kudos to the master of war scribes'—**Anand Ranganathan, professor, Special Centre for Molecular Medicine, Jawaharlal Nehru University**

'Bhaavna has a very visual style of writing and her ability of capturing the smallest detail in her storytelling style makes this book a very compelling read'—**Samar Khan, film director, producer and CEO, Juggernaut Productions**

'In *Nagrota Under Siege*, Bhaavna Arora brings to the reader the little-known story of the terrorist attack by the Jaish-e-Mohammed on 29 November 2016. Her extraordinary understanding of the way

Pakistani terrorists operate in Jammu and Kashmir and her detailed research unravel in vivid detail what happened on that unfortunate day. She has, with her unerring woman's instinct, homed in on the emotional aspects of the stories of each of the Indian protagonists, bringing all of them to a head at the final showdown, showcasing the part played by each of the seven intrepid warriors who made the ultimate sacrifice. Of special importance is her understanding of the trauma experienced by the families of the heroes, who watched with bated breath as the story unfolded in the media. In this, Maj. Akshay Girish's story assumes special significance because of the heroic manner in which he carried out his death-defying duty right to the very end and the stoic manner in which his parents have accepted his sacrifice on the platform of national honour. A very engaging story that needs to be read by every Indian citizen'—**Maj. Gen. Ian Cardozo, AVSM, SM (retd), war hero and disabled soldier**

'It reads like a racy thriller with many characters linked together in a cross-border terror attack. The only difference is it is all fact and no fiction. This book by Bhaavna Arora is her best yet. Feel the emotions and pride in the Indian Army'—**Maj. Dr Surendra Poonia, VSM (retd),** *Limca Book of Records* **record holder; physician and former Special Forces officer, Indian Army; and founder, Soldierathon marathon and Fit Bharat**

'Bhaavna Arora narrates in a suspenseful and nerve-racking manner the ordeal of the soldiers and families who went through the incident (the attack on the officers' mess complex). She has woven and unfolded the entire incident of 29 November 2016 extremely well. Her narration showcases research and a deep understanding of the human side of the people she writes about. The book also reflects her love and adulation for the army and our country. My compliments to Bhaavna, who is an army brat, for having the courage to research and write on the Nagrota fidayeen attack. She has shown deep involvement and passion in writing this book in spite of many hurdles. The book is a masterpiece and I recommend it to all, especially the men in uniform'—**Lt Gen. Ajae Kumar Sharma, UYSM, YSM, SM (retd); former corps commander, XVI Corps; and former state information commissioner, Punjab**

NAGROTA UNDER SIEGE

bhaavna arora

PENGUIN
VEER

An imprint of Penguin Random House

PENGUIN VEER

USA | Canada | UK | Ireland | Australia
New Zealand | India | South Africa | China | Singapore

Penguin Veer is an imprint of the Penguin Random House group of companies
whose addresses can be found at global.penguinrandomhouse.com

Published by Penguin Random House India Pvt. Ltd
4th Floor, Capital Tower 1, MG Road,
Gurugram 122 002, Haryana, India

First published in Penguin Veer by Penguin Random House India 2024

10 9 8 7 6 5 4 3 2

This book is a work of non-fiction. The views and opinions expressed in the book are
those of the author only and do not reflect or represent the views and opinions held
by any other person. This book is based on a variety of sources, including published
materials and research conducted by the author, and on interviews and interactions of
the author with the persons mentioned in the manuscript. It reflects the author's own
understanding and conception of such materials and/or can be verified by research. All
persons within the book are actual individuals and the names and characteristics of
some individuals have been changed to respect their privacy. The objective of this book
is not to hurt any sentiments or be biased in favour of or against any particular person,
political party, region, caste, society, gender, creed, nation or religion.

Please note that no part of this book may be used or reproduced in any manner
for the purpose of training artificial intelligence technologies or systems.

ISBN 9780143470656

Typeset in Adobe Caslon Pro by MAP Systems, Bengaluru, India
Printed at Repro India Limited

www.penguin.co.in

This is a legitimate digitally printed version of the book and therefore might not
have certain extra finishing on the cover.

To Lieutenant General P.C. Thimayya, PVSM,
VSM (retd):
In a world where trust can feel rare, your faith in me has been nothing short of transformative. It is your trust that has allowed stories of valour, Indian nationalism and patriotism to find their voice. Your support has been the foundation upon which this book stands, and for that, I am forever grateful.

To the courageous soldiers and families who were part of the Nagrota attack:
This book is dedicated to your unbreakable spirit and sacrifice. Your stories of bravery are the heart of this narrative, a tribute to those who stood fearlessly in the face of unimaginable challenges.

To the soldiers who gave their all, who fought with the utmost courage and who laid down their lives in the line of duty:
You are remembered here. This is for you, the heroes who protect us with selfless devotion.

To every mother, father, wife, sister, daughter and brother who has lost a beloved one to terrorism:
Your loss is a reminder of the unseen battles you carry daily. This dedication holds your strength, resilience and the stories of those you loved and lost.

And, finally, to the soldiers of the Indian Army:
Thank you. Every page of this book is a testament to your courage, honour and the sacrifices you make to keep us safe. We owe you more than words can convey.

Contents

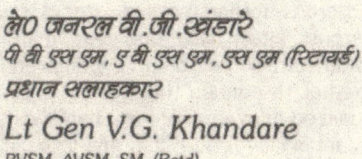

ले0 जनरल वी.जी.खंडारे
पी वी एस एम, ए वी एस एम, एस एम (रिटायर्ड)
प्रधान सलाहकार

Lt Gen V.G. Khandare
PVSM, AVSM, SM, (Retd)

भारत सरकार
नई दिल्ली - 110 011
Government of India
Ministry of Defence
New Dehi-110 011

FOREWORD

Great stories are written when the blood shed by brave and patriotic soldiers mixes with the ink of gifted and equally patriotic authors.

Proud mothers send their sons and daughters to the great Indian Army and they continue to smile with pride through the unimaginable pain even after they have sacrificed all in their silent endeavor to keep the nation safe. These mothers are braver than many like me who have fought in actual wars and conflicts on the borders and in the hinterland against fanatics.

Wives of soldiers who lose their husbands combating terrorism or fighting in conventional wars have to move ahead in life without their beloved holding their hand; they are no less courageous than the combatant in uniform.

The innocent and lovely children of these brave warriors grow up through all odds, without their fathers or mothers all because they believe the honour and safety of the nation always comes first. They grow up with memories of their parent's patriotism and national pride as children much before they become adults.

The officers and soldiers who sacrificed their lives in action fighting bravely and the ones who survived that fight during the Nagrota attack were waiting for the story of their valour to be told. The nation also deserves to know every bit of this real-life heroism. Army values and ethos stand firmly at the core of it all. We live for the nation, we kill for the nation without any personal agenda, and we die for our citizens, for our future generation and especially for the sake of our national honour.

- 2 -

Pakistan-sponsored cross-border terrorist attacks are not new for India and Nagrota terrorist attack was one among them. It was, in many ways, similar to others and yet, also very different. The way the entire team came together to contain the OGWs who supported the fidayeens. These radicalized fidayeens are the handiwork of Pakistan's ISI, radicalized Pakistani military and the anti-India elements from Pakistani society, whose only dream is to bleed India through a thousand cuts. It is shameful to see Indian sleeper cells falling prey to these evil designs. It is to the credit of our heroes that India has thwarted Pakistan's evil designs to break up India or to subjugate Indians.

Last but not least, I would like to congratulate the author Bhaavna Arora for successfully bringing to light the story of the Nagrota terror attack through this very well researched and factually narrated thriller.

I wish the book all the success it richly deserves.

(ले. जनरल विनोद जी खंडारे)
(Lt. Gen. Vinod G Khandare)
प्रधान सलाहकार / Principal Adviser
रक्षा मंत्रालय / Ministry of Defence
नई दिल्ली / New Delhi

A Note to My Readers

This book is not a work of fiction but a story based on successive research on an attack that took place in 2016 in the Nagrota cantonment by three Jaish-e-Mohammed fidayeens.

All characters and incidents in this work are real. There is an absolute resemblance to the people living or dead and it is coincidental.

I claim every responsibility or liability for any errors or omissions.

This piece of work is not solely for entertainment but to sensitize my readers to the sacrifices our armed forces make towards keeping us safe. I have given five years of my life to bring this story to you.

I have performed my prescribed duties without expecting any fruits of my actions.

While working, I gave up the pride of doership.

I offer my work to God, I offer my work to my readers.

'I did my best!'

—A soldier

'I was there to see it!'

—A buddy

'I'm here to write about it!'

—An author

What good is a sacrifice if not chronicled?

Prologue

As Meghna walked quietly to the site where her son had been found in a pool of blood, her heart started pounding. She had loved her son and still did. As she walked to the spot she would later call *karambhoomi*, or the land of reckoning, she was reminded of how unwavering her son, Major Akshay Girish, had been in following his childhood dream. She was accompanied by Lieutenant Colonel Ravi Raina as well as her husband Girish and their daughter Neha. Neha was Akshay's twin and was feeling a sense of acute loss that is unique to a twin sibling; like a phantom limb, it was a pain that was more sensed than felt. Neha's husband, Pradish and Akshay's widow Sangeeta had also insisted on coming along. Meghna didn't know what she would have done without them by her side.

Her thoughts took her back to her son's short life. 'Akshay, *mera raja beta*,' is what she had called him his whole life. Her beloved son, a prince among men. She closed her eyes and remembered the words Akshay had written to her in his last letter:

If you feel alone, think of me. I can't promise I will be in front of you, but when you close your eyes, you will see me.

At the time, she had never imagined that these words were going to carry such a deep meaning for her for the rest of her life. She opened her eyes and a tear trickled down her cheek. When she had planned her trip to Nagrota, she had told herself that she'd be strong, just as her son would have wanted her to be. She had made a promise to herself and to her son that she would not cry.

She walked on, remembering the courageous men and women who had been trapped, and the stories about those who had rescued them on the morning of 29 November 2016. Men and women as courageous as her son.

She had travelled all the way from Bengaluru looking for answers to questions she never had the heart to ask. There seemed to be a cosmic pull asking her to visit the place where her son had fought bravely, and given up his young life.

'My daddy went to heaven after getting hurt fighting bad uncles,' Naina, her three-year-old granddaughter, would heartbreakingly describe the loss of her father.

The mother, who had had sleepless nights at the thought of her son's slightest discomfort, was now looking for something in his karambhoomi that she could cling to and live on. Something that would add meaning to the rest of her life. As a mother, it would be her goal to live for the child who had been taken away fighting for a nation he loved.

Lt Col Raina halted beside a building with a staircase. He turned to Meghna, who had stopped as well, 'Ma'am, this was where Akshay was found.' Meghna's heart skipped a beat and for a moment she froze.

It was sensitive of Ravi to have said, 'where Akshay was found' rather than saying, 'where Akshay's body was found'.

She pretended to be stoic, acutely aware that the soldiers who had also lost their brothers-in-arms were watching the family's every reaction. But being brave on the outside was easier than unscrambling the feelings that were tearing her apart inside. She walked ahead, bent down and picked up a pebble from the place Ravi had pointed to. It would be a reminder of Akshay's sacrifice.

At that very moment, Pradish, who had been taking pictures of the site, stumbled upon a pair of glasses on the ground. He quickly came towards Meghna and the younger women. 'Do these belong to Akshay?' he asked, placing the glasses in Sangeeta's hands as Neha turned around to look at the proffered glasses.

The newly widowed young woman looked at the glasses in her hands and brought them close to her chest. It was almost like she had found Akshay again and he was saying, 'I see you, Sangeeta, I will always see you.'

'Yes, these are Akshay's!' she said, her eyes welling up.

Ravi looked at the glasses and was surprised beyond belief at how the army and the National Investigation Agency (NIA) had missed them during the investigation of the site. He considered it nothing short of a miracle, as the NIA's investigative team had cut bushes and dug out mud at every corner of that site in order to gather evidence for a thorough investigation.

'Ma'am, it was as if Akshay wanted you to find them,' Ravi proclaimed.

Teary-eyed Meghna looked at Ravi with deep sadness. There was nothing to be done. It was a moment of acceptance. Of final acceptance that her son was gone. The three women hugged each other and wept their hearts out, their tears falling on Akshay's muddied glasses. Their tears didn't rule out the fact that they were all courageous women. For each of them, Akshay's passing was an irreparable loss. Each one had lost a bit of herself in his death.

The careful delusion each one had built of it all being a bad dream, one that each secretly hoped they'd wake up from, came crashing down around them. Akshay was definitely gone. What was left behind was a story waiting to be told.

Chapter 1

On the Trail of a Lost Mobile

'Sir, I didn't steal that phone. It was just lying abandoned on the road,' Zakir kept pleading with the constable who had arrested him. A foreign tourist from Vatican City had registered a complaint about his lost mobile phone two days ago.

After the monster of terrorism had raised its ugly head and spread its tentacles across the Kashmir Valley, tourism in the state had hit an all-time low. The steep downfall started in July 1995 when six foreigners—two Britons, two Americans, one German and a Norwegian actor—were kidnapped by members of the terrorist organization Harkat-ul-Mujahideen, now known as Jaish-e-Mohammed (JeM). After Harkat-ul-Mujahideen was banned in 1999, their leader, Masood Azhar, went on to form JeM. They made many illegitimate demands from the Indian government, including Azhar's release. He had been arrested by the government in February 1994. In August 1995, one of those six foreigners was found beheaded after the Indian government refused

1

to heed the terrorists' demands. Though one of victims managed to escape, no one ever heard from the remaining four hostages. The news was splashed across international media and as a result, tourism in Jammu and Kashmir suffered terribly.

* * *

In a troubled atmosphere charged with violence, fear and insecurity, the police and the administration had an enormous responsibility to take care of tourists as they were easy targets. It was, therefore, expected that even a petty crime like that of a mobile phone theft would be taken seriously by the police.

'Sir, if you let me go, I have a piece of information that can get you promoted to a sub-inspector,' Zakir tried to subtly bribe the constable.

'Keep your mouth shut!' the constable shouted at his catch.

'Sir, you have to believe me,' Zakir pleaded again.

'Will you keep quiet? Else, I'll kick your balls!' the constable angrily got up from his chair.

But after a few minutes, Zakir was still singing the same tune, 'Sir, this information can change your life.'

That aroused the constable's curiosity and he wanted to know what Zakir had to say. Most of the police operations ran on networks and the information they provided. Though there were special anti-terror cells in Jammu and Kashmir, due to the density of terrorist activities, every police station and police personnel were either formally, or occasionally informally, trained to handle such situations.

The constable held Zakir by the scruff of his neck and violently shook him, warning, 'I'll break your teeth if I find you wasting my time.'

Zakir could see trouble staring in his face and without hesitating, he meekly capitulated, 'Sir, I've some information. Two pistols and a few grenades.'

It was not the first time that Zakir had stolen such phones. But from the constable's menacing attitude, he realized that the police were taking the security of foreign tourists very seriously. He therefore thought it prudent to share a vital piece of information with the police to save himself from rotting in jail.

***

Knowing that it was binding on him to pass that information to his senior, the constable rushed to the circle inspector who was busy talking to a tourist. 'Tourists usually don't come to this side of town. What were you doing in Khanyar?'

'Sir, I had longed to visit the Roza Bal shrine. You may surely be knowing that Mirza Ghulam Ahmad claimed the shrine is actually the tomb of Jesus and I'm a Catholic. Though I believe that the whole tomb thing is a hoax, a lot of people claim that global warming is also a hoax,' the tourist shrugged.

Listening to their conversation, the constable looked at the inspector pointedly to convey that he was neither interested in Jesus nor in global warming. He had a more pressing issue at hand, which had to be dealt with by his senior and without any delay.

The constable bent down and whispered in the inspector's ear, 'Sir, two pistols and a few grenades.'

* * *

Though the inspector's eyes widened at the startling revelation, he smiled looking at the tourist who was curious about what had transpired between the two police officials. The inspector tried to disguise his astonishment with a smile but had little success.

'Sir, I've got my phone back and don't want anything else. If you suggest, I can take my complaint back.' The tourist looked at the inspector, waiting for his response. He didn't get any, so he left saying, 'Sir, it's not so much about the phone as the data in it. Thank you for being so helpful.'

He wanted to get out of the inspector's hair, sensing the urgency that seemed to have suddenly filled the room.

'It's absolutely your choice, my friend. If you want the man to be punished, we are with you. Your well-being is our only concern.'

The inspector sounded politically and legally correct. The tourist chose to leave the police station with his phone so that he could continue holidaying without wasting any more time.

* * *

As soon as the tourist left, the inspector got up from his chair and ran towards Zakir who was squatting in a corner of the lock-up. He pulled Zakir up by the collar, slapped him twice and screamed, 'You think we are fools sitting here? I'll cut you to pieces if you don't tell me the truth.'

'Sir, I'll tell you only if you let me walk free afterwards. I just picked up a mobile that was lying on the ground, while you have people with pistols and grenades on the loose.'

'When and where did you find it?' the inspector was now getting down to specifics.

'Will you set me free after that, sir?' Zakir pleaded with folded hands.

The inspector slapped him again, and this time so hard, that Zakir peed his pants. The police were quite used to this type of a drill across the country so it came as no surprise to the inspector. But it did establish the fact that Zakir was not a seasoned criminal. And the inspector knew that a seasoned criminal would never barter information about arms in exchange for a reprieve from a mobile phone theft.

'Should I put a diaper on him, sir?' the constable asked the inspector seriously. There were times when petty criminals not only peed, but also soiled their pants.

* * *

Aware that the inspector was serious about interrogating him, Zakir wasn't sure if he was striking the right deal. The inspector raised his hand to slap him again when he blurted out the address where he had seen the weapons.

The inspector sat in the chair facing Zakir and threatened him, 'I'll annihilate your entire breed if you're lying.'

In order to be thorough with the investigation, the constable started digging out information on Zakir. He spoke to the people on Zakir's mobile contact list. He then told his senior about the information he had gathered about Zakir, 'Sir, he is an orphan and has no criminal history. He is mostly seen in and around Lal Chowk, outside a shawl shop, luring tourists to buy fake Pashmina.'

Zakir meekly intervened, 'Sir, for every customer who buys Pashmina with my guidance, I get a 2 per cent commission.'

'So, that's exactly how he got his hands on the phone, sir,' the constable reaffirmed.

'I'm least interested in the phone and his damn business. Tell me what were you doing in that place?' the inspector shouted.

'Sir, I was offered money to hurl grenades at a police station,' Zakir said quickly. He knew that only one thing could save him now and that was the truth.

The inspector and the constable exchanged shocked looks and thundered in one voice,

'Which police station?'

Zakir looked at the floor without answering. The constable kicked him and asked again, 'You bastard! Which police station?'

Zakir screamed in pain and pointed at the signboard—'PS Khanyar'—the police station that they were presently sitting in.

The constable looked at the inspector and kicked Zakir again, shouting, 'Bastard! Wanted to blow our asses, sir!'

* * *

The local militants would often look for soft targets like Zakir who were vulnerable, and carried either emotional or physical baggage, or were simply devoid of financial or familial support, to carry out such local terror activities.

'Who is that man?' the inspector looked at Zakir as though he'd swallow him.

'His name is Umar Bashir but locals call him Chachoo,' Zakir blurted out. His quick replies indicated he was being truthful.

'Get our team ready. We are going to meet Chachoo,' the inspector ordered.

'Sir, what about an arrest warrant? Search warrant?' the constable reminded his boss of the legal procedure. But his boss gave him a disgusted look and asked him to follow him.

They drove out in a bulletproof vehicle with the police team. The team also took Zakir along so that they didn't waste time looking for Chachoo.

* * *

Zakir led them to Chachoo's house, and when no one opened the door after some knocking, they broke it open and started searching the house. Zakir directed them towards a bedroom and bent down to open a bed box. The bed box contained more ammunition than what Zakir had divulged.

Chachoo, who was enjoying a siesta in his backyard, was rudely awakened by the commotion in the house, and ran towards his bedroom to find a team of police officials collecting the ammunition after taking pictures of it. When his eyes fell on Zakir, he realized that he was in big trouble. He tried to run but was arrested and handcuffed.

* * *

Once the team was back at the police station, the interrogation began.

'Where did you get this ammunition?' the inspector asked tersely.

Chachoo couldn't deny anything or feign ignorance as the ammunition had been found right inside his house, in his bed box.

'Sir, Munir-ul-Hassan Qadri had given me two pistols,' Chachoo said without mincing words.

'From where did Munir get all this?' the inspector asked and was shocked when he heard Chachoo say, 'From across the border.'

The case had to be transferred to the Cargo police station that dealt with any kind of terrorist activity taking place in J&K. Munir's phone was put on surveillance and before he knew it, he was picked up by the police from his house in HMT, Mohalla Mughal Darbar, in Srinagar on 23 April 2018.

It was the moment when a ghastly sequence of events written in blood started unravelling.

* * *

SSP Hamid Ansari* had been recently posted to Cargo police station and was enjoying every bit of his tenure there. His seniors, DIG Rahmatulla Gurbaz and IG Ahmed Khan, asked him to interrogate Munir. During the preliminary investigation, the SSP established that the case

---

* The names of the officers have been changed for security reasons as they are still in service.

was far more serious than it appeared to be. There were bigger predators navigating the border.

The SSP went to the DIG with all the information he had gathered about Munir and briefed his senior, 'Sir, in September 1990, Syed Munir-ul-Hassan Qadri had crossed the LoC (Line of Control) and gone to Muzaffarabad in Pakistan-occupied Kashmir (PoK). He started living there with his distant relatives. His cousin had taken him to Al-Barq camp and he had a close association with the training camps for terrorists there.'

The DIG wasn't surprised at the information. In his entire career as a top cop in J&K, he had often come across such people. In the 1990s, many Kashmiris had gone to PoK in search of greener pastures but the economic condition of the people there was much worse. The Kashmiris there had got the status of refugees and had to live in camps as there was no proper housing. In the name of housing, there were only temporary structures made of mud, tin or bricks.

'When did he come back to India?' The DIG didn't ask 'why' as he knew the reasons quite well.

'Sir, he returned via Nepal in August 2011 during implementation of the rehabilitation policy of terrorists. He doesn't have a passport and has a wife and two or three children,' the SSP gave more details.

'If he doesn't have a passport, he can't travel. That means he might have had another accomplice with a passport who would have helped him. He is not alone. Dig out his phone details.'

The DIG was speaking from his vast experience.

'Yes, sir.' The SSP nodded in agreement and left after taking orders from his senior.

* * *

Munir didn't divulge any information for around two weeks. He was seemingly a hard nut to crack. He did speak about his life in Muzaffarabad and the difficulties there, to gain sympathy, but the J&K police had the reputation of being not only tough but also patient.

'I don't have a job, sir. I can barely make both ends meet. I have tried to raise this issue many times with the J&K administration about the plight of the refugees but no one cares. I know the president of the rehabilitation centre, Dharmendra Sharma. I also know some people in Delhi, sir, who know what I'm fighting for . . .' Munir went on and on until the SSP interrupted him. 'What are you fighting for?' the police officer asked, dropping a seed of doubt in Munir's mind.

Munir was silent and tried to figure out a convincing answer that would help his case, but couldn't. Was he fighting for the rights of the refugees? Was he fighting for jihad or was he just trying to make both ends meet? He was confused and had never expected to end up in jail like this.

* * *

'In what capacity did you work in Tariq Ahmad Dar's company?'

Munir had expected that question from the SSP but didn't think it would come so soon.

When the impatient SSP repeated the same question in a graver tone, Munir revealed, 'I got a job in his company in 2015 and since then, I've been looking after the timber business of his company that goes by the name Akash Timber.'

'What do you do?' the SSP inquired.

'Everything, sir, from the procurement of wood to the distribution of furniture,' Munir replied.

***

The SSP knew that he couldn't summon Tariq until there was solid evidence against him. And so, he started digging for more information from Munir.

He returned to a more valid and pertinent question, 'From where did you get these pistols?'

Munir refused to talk. When criminals like Munir refuse to talk, the police use a lot of traditional techniques like isolation and maximization where police personnel play good cop, and minimization where the same or different police personnel play bad cop. Fortunately, those techniques worked on Munir and he started talking, 'Sir, these pistols don't belong to me.'

'To whom then?'

The SSP was just waiting for Munir to reveal another name. He was sure, as was the DIG, that Munir couldn't have done anything alone. Until then, they were not even sure what Munir and his team had done. But the recovery of pistols and grenades was a big deal.

'They belong to Ashiq Baba. I was there when he gave them to Chachoo, but I have no idea from where he got them,' Munir said. He knew that he was in big trouble and the only way he could get his jail term reduced was by giving the names of people who were involved with him, to the police.

'Give us his mobile number along with Tariq's,' the SSP ordered. Munir complied, scribbled their mobile numbers on a piece of paper and handed it over to the SSP.

The SSP, in turn, passed it over to his team and ordered, 'Get the history and geography of these numbers. *Saari kundali nikalo inki.*'

* * *

The next day, the investigating team handed over a file to the SSP containing all the details of both the numbers. It was established from the details that Munir, Tariq and Ashiq had been in constant touch with each other through those numbers since December 2016. That was an interesting fact and a revelation of prime importance for the SSP.

The SSP ordered his men to bring Munir in.

After a few minutes, when Munir appeared before the SSP, he was asked, 'I want to know about the mobile numbers that you three were using before December 2016.'

The SSP didn't ask why because he didn't want to waste time on fantasies that Munir would have woven in his mind in order to get away with the crime. He wanted to validate everything with technical data. A human being can lie a thousand times, but technology always reveals the truth and the SSP was desperate to find the truth behind those pistols.

'Sir, those numbers are no longer in use,' Munir justified.

'You think I don't know that? I won't let you get away before giving me complete details about those mobile numbers,' SSP Hamid threatened Munir.

'It's better you cooperate with SSP *saab* if you want your sentence to be reduced or you'll have all sorts of charges against you. Chachoo has already given testimony against you,' one of the team members whispered in Munir's ear after the SSP had left.

***

Munir had been in police custody for two weeks, including his remand period. He knew that he was guilty of a crime that was bigger than what police knew of at the moment. He tried to pin it completely on Ashiq Baba. 'Sir, please question Ashiq Baba. You'll get to know his involvement in this entire case,' Munir begged the SSP.

'For that, you'll have to give me more information.'

The SSP was trying to play good cop.

Munir decided to open up in order to save his skin and disclosed, 'Sir, Ashiq has been visiting Pakistan and PoK since 2015. You can check his passport.'

'So? Many people visit Pakistan. What's the big deal?' The SSP clearly wanted more.

'Sir, during his visit, he met Malik Safdar, a driver working with Jaish-e-Mohammed. Malik arranged a meeting with Waseem who is the operational commander of JeM, Abu Talha aka Doctor who is the detachment (det) commander and Qari Zarar who is the launching commander of JeM for the Jammu region.'

The SSP and his team exchanged astonished looks. 'How do I know you're telling the truth?' the SSP probed further.

'Sir, bring him in with his mobile phone. Not the one with his present number but the one he used before December 2016.'

Handing over a pen and a piece of paper to Munir, the SSP ordered, 'Give me that number . . . write it down.'

* * *

The SSP took Munir's confession to the DIG. After handing over the confessional statement to his superior, he asked, 'Sir, seeking your permission. Can we pick up Ashiq?'

'Ashiq Baba? Aloochibagh, Srinagar?' The DIG was shocked to hear his name.

'Do we know him, sir?' The SSP was surprised at his boss's reaction.

'He was our informer. We have acted many times on his information to save a number of disasters. What has he done?' The DIG was obviously not happy to know that their informer had double-crossed the police.

'Sir, we'll know once we bring him here.'

* * *

Ashiq was picked up from his house and brought to the police station in no time. The DIG was present to 'welcome' him.

'What did you do, Ashiq? I thought you were on our side.'

The DIG was now a part of the interrogation team.

Ashiq kept standing with his head bowed in front of the police officers. 'I needed money for the treatment of my wife, sir. She is dying,' Ashiq started crying.

'Who gave you those pistols?' the DIG shouted. He had never spoken that rudely and Ashiq was mortally scared.

'Sir, I was not the only one,' Ashiq sobbed.

'Who were the others?'

The SSP was eager to know while the DIG was anxious about 'how' Ashiq got those pistols.

'Tariq Ahmad Dar, Munir-ul-Hassan and Ashraf Hamid Khandey,' Ashiq mumbled.

The DIG grilled, 'What did you all do?' The SSP went through Ashiq's mobile phone.

He found pictures of Ashiq at the office of the Hizbul Mujahideen headed by Syed Salhauddin at Link Road in Islamabad in 2016.

The SSP brought the phone to his boss and started swiping the pictures one by one, commenting, 'Sir, look at this photograph . . . here he is meeting Qari Zarar. And in this, he can be seen with Mufti Asgar, the launching commander of JeM. They all are definitely involved in something bigger. Either it has already happened or is about to happen.'

'It has already happened, Hamid, and if it was about to happen, then it won't happen now.' The DIG knew this from experience.

'Sir, Munir and Tariq were the masterminds behind this. They got the fidayeens from across the border who handed over the pistols to them. Tariq gave those pistols to Chachoo. I was not involved at all. Believe me, sir,' Ashiq pleaded.

'Where are the fidayeens now?'

Ashiq realized that he had given away too much information, but a guilty conscience has nowhere to hide.

'When did you get them here?' The DIG was now clenching his teeth with anger. When Ashiq didn't answer, the DIG ordered the SSP, 'Pull out their bank details. If they've aided an infiltration, there is sure to be a wired transaction for the same. Trace it.'

'Sir, let me kick his balls twice, he will say everything like a parrot!' The SSP sought his boss's permission, who advised him, 'You'll still need evidence to prove it.'

***

Ashiq's grilling continued and after they managed to extract a considerable amount of information from him, the SSP and DIG went to Inspector General of Police Ahmed Khan, to brief him about the case.

'Sir, it is an established fact that Munir, Tariq, Ashiq and Khandey were involved in providing local aid to the terrorists who had attacked the Nagrota Army Camp on 29 November 2016.'

***

The DIG gave his senior more details about the case. The IG had been in service longer than the DIG and the SSP, and without a doubt, had more contacts and networks. So, telling him about the case made things move faster. The IG was a decorated officer and had served with the DIG in south Kashmir. They were both aware that Ashiq was an informant for them.

'Why did he go rogue on us?' the IG inquired.

'I believe his wife is suffering from cancer and he needed money for her treatment,' the DIG replied.

'What a waste of an asset!' The IG shook his head and continued in a disappointed tone, 'Anyway, go ahead with the investigation and as soon as you find any inkling of Tariq's involvement, take him into custody.'

After thinking for a few minutes, the IG asked again, 'What about the fourth boy?'

'We are trying to establish a link, sir,' DIG Gurbaz replied.

When IG Khan signalled the meeting had ended, he exhorted, 'All the best and keep the NIA in the picture.' The DIG and the SSP noted their senior's command and left after saluting him.

Chapter 2

Terror Sneaks Across

Munir-ul-Hassan Qadri started working for Tariq Ahmad Dar in 2015. After a few months, he came in contact with Ashiq Baba who wanted to trade in Pakistan. In the aftermath of the September 2014 floods in Kashmir, when his job of setting up of solar lights came to an end, Ashiq started looking for other avenues to make both ends meet. Munir had developed many contacts in Pakistan during his eleven-year-long stay in Muzaffarabad. He was in touch with Waseem, the operation and det commander of JeM. The contacts that Munir passed on to Ashiq were not just for trading spices and dry fruits but also for trading information and dealing with terrorists.

* * *

Ashiq did go to Pakistan in 2016, but traded that information for the Indian side. He made sure to win the trust of the J&K police on the basis of that information. Within a year, Munir had built enough trust in terms of handling Tariq's money

and running his organization. In July 2016, after the death
of Burhan Wani, the much-wanted poster boy of terrorism
of Kashmir, Tariq's business took a hit and he suffered huge
losses. Soon, Munir came to know that Tariq's company was
facing a loss of over Rs 9 crore that had to be paid soon.
The banks were threatening Tariq to confiscate his property
and house. His brother-in-law's property had also been
mortgaged for the business. Tariq was helpless and on the
brink of losing his sanity. With Munir joining his company,
Tariq saw a ray of hope because he was able to make a partial
payment to the bank in one year. That enabled Tariq to buy
some more time to pay the rest.

* * *

When Ashiq discovered that his wife was suffering from
cancer, he knew had to make more money and that too
quickly, for her treatment. He decided to play for the other
side and a proposal came his way from Waseem. He was
deputed to facilitate the infiltration of three fidayeens to
India and was promised a sum of Rs 30 lakh in return. He
discussed it with Munir and both of them snagged the deal.
For Munir and Ashiq, it was not so much about the money
as about their loyalties towards jihad and Pakistan. Having
worked for Tariq for almost a year, Munir knew that he
could be exploited for money. So, he threw a bone of Rs 2
crore to Tariq and he became a part of the plan.

'What are we supposed to do?' Tariq inquired.

'Tariq *mian*, we've just to get three men from across the
border and hand them over to the commissioner of police

in Delhi who will carry out their encounter. And we will get money in return for our *services*.' Munir was lying, but in Kashmir anything is believed.

'Don't you think it's illegal?' a visibly terrified Tariq asked.

'What is illegal when the police are involved, sir? You have to trust me. Has your vehicle ever got held up at the toll?'

By then, Tariq knew that Munir had good contacts as he had been running his business successfully. While trading information, he had built a rapport with important people in Kashmir, especially the police. With that background, Munir and Ashiq were only hoodwinking the police.

* * *

In the first week of November, Munir, Ashiq and Tariq had a meeting to chalk out their further course of action.

'I've been called by the commissioner to come to Delhi to discuss the plan,' Munir told his partners in crime.

'Will the encounter take place in Delhi?' Tariq asked as he had by then started to believe Munir's story.

'We aren't sure, Tariq bhai. Such serious matters aren't discussed openly. Only the top commanders know what the plan is. We'll do what we are expected to and get our money.'

Tariq didn't look very convinced as he was scared of the fallout of a crime of such magnitude. But the promise of that kind of money was enough to lure him into agreement. On 16 November 2016, Munir travelled to Delhi to get a brief on the plan from the Pakistani messengers and was back in Jammu after four days.

At that time, Ashiq was on his way to Manashera in Pakistan to undergo training in handling communication gadgets, including wireless sets, mobile phones and GPS.

***

After meeting people in Delhi, Munir took a flight to Jammu on 20 November 2016 and checked into Hotel Jagdamba. Munir asked Ashiq to join him there. On 22 November, Ashiq drove his Hyundai i10 car from Srinagar to reach the hotel in Jammu where Munir was staying.

'We need to conduct a recce of the coordinates given by Wasim.' Ashiq wanted to get to work without losing any time.

'How many people are they sending?' Munir asked.

'Three,' Ashiq held up as many fingers.

'Let's wait tonight. By then I'll also ask Tariq to join us. Your vehicle is not spacious enough to carry all the men and the ammunition.'

'Okay,' Ashiq nodded.

Munir called Tariq, 'We need to meet at Jagdamba hotel in Jammu, Tariq bhai. Come with your car.'

'When?' Tariq inquired.

'Just come. We've no time to waste.' Munir hung up after short instructions.

***

Tariq left for Jammu the next day. He took Hamid Khandey with him to drive his car because he didn't want to go alone. He was scared. Before Tariq and Khandey reached Jammu, Ashiq and Munir left in their Hyundai i10 to check the Nagrota Army Camp. They wanted to do a recce of the place before they deputed the three terrorists do their job. Khandey and Tariq took less than six hours to reach Hotel Jagdamba and join Munir and Ashiq in the room they were staying in.

'Why did you bring him?' Munir asked Tariq, pointing at Khandey.

'To be honest, I was scared to drive all the way alone,' Tariq admitted.

'It's all right. But he doesn't need to know,' Ashiq instructed.

'Doesn't need to know what?' Khandey was getting curious and restless too.

'We're planning to start a new business and for that, we're looking at some places. We will be doing a recce of those places tomorrow.' Ashiq wanted to throw a cloak on the satanic plan that was underway.

'Let's rest tonight and start our work tomorrow?' Munir looked at his accomplices for approval. The meeting dispersed and all four left for their respective rooms for the night.

* * *

The next day, 24 November, all four left to see the army camp and also locate the three other GPS locations marked by the JeM commanders for receiving the terrorists. Ashiq had all the three locations in his mobile phone. They first went to the Motta Khad bridge. Munir and Ashiq got out of their car to verify the coordinates with the WhatsApp location shared with them. They did the same for the second location near Tarnah bridge on NHW 44, with Khandey and Tariq following them. The third location was towards a link road that led from Dyalachak to Hiranagar near an army camp. Munir and Ashiq got off at the army camp and started taking pictures and videos.

* * *

'Tariq bhai, what are they doing?' Khandey, who was in the driver's seat with Tariq in his Mahindra Verito, was now getting suspicious.

'Don't worry,' Tariq was scared but tried to reassure Khandey.

Though there was no contact with the JeM handlers on the mobile phone, Ashiq knew that the three terrorists were arriving on the 26th evening. So they all left for Motta Khad bridge from Hotel Jagdamba and waited there until the morning of the 27th. On seeing no sign of the terrorists, they left the place and returned to the hotel.

'What do we do now?' Munir asked Ashiq who was better trained by the JeM, though Munir has also attended terrorists' camps when he was in PoK.

'I've got to break into a Wi-Fi network to get in touch with Waseem in Pakistan.' Ashiq knew that it was most important to get in touch with Waseem.

Ashiq and Munir went to KC Plaza, Jammu and Ashiq cracked the Wi-Fi password and WhatsApped Waseem:

The plan is delayed by a day. The code name you'll use will be 'Amir' and our freedom fighters will reply to that with 'Qasim'. I suggest you get some blankets and a wire cutter from a market before you pick them up. They will be in uniforms so make sure you get some civilian clothes they can change into.

* * *

After getting instructions on WhatsApp from Waseem, Ashiq and Munir went to Jewel Chowk and picked up all the necessary items the terrorists would need for the operation from different costermongers. The next day, 28 November, they arrived at Motta Khad bridge with Ashiq and Munir in the Hyundai i10 driven by Ashiq. The Verito was driven by Khandey with Tariq as the passenger. They had left at four in the morning. They parked their cars at a distance from Motta Khad bridge. Ashiq alone got out of the car and instructed his accomplices, 'Just stay here. You'll get a signal the moment I get them.'

Ashiq then took a bag containing civilian clothes and blankets for the three terrorists and left. He went down to the bridge and saw three men in army combat uniforms smeared in mud carrying weapons and backpacks. Ashiq offered the bag containing clothes only after confirming their identity with the exchange of codes—'Amir' and 'Qasim'. The three terrorists—Khalid, Numan and Aadil— hurriedly changed into the clothes Ashiq had brought, who took their muddy uniforms and put them in the bag. After taking out the blankets, Ashiq asked them to keep their weapons under cover. The three terrorists and Ashiq came up to the bridge and Ashiq gestured to Munir, Tariq and Khandey to come ahead with the vehicles.

* * *

Tariq was driving the Mahindra Verito while Khandey followed him in the i10 with Munir sitting next to him. The three terrorists got inside the Verito after putting their bags and ammunition in the boot. They drove to the hotel.

* * *

'Can we stop somewhere to have a cup of tea?' Aadil requested Ashiq.

Realizing that the three men had been on their feet over the last few days and were hungry, Ashiq called up Munir and asked him to stop at the next tea stall on the highway. They stopped at Sharma tea stall at Gurha Mundian.

In his heart of hearts, Tariq felt a deep pity for the terrorists as he knew they were going to be killed soon in a police encounter. All of them were silent while sipping tea at the stall. Though each of their actions was prompted by a different motive, they had two things in common—angst against the Indian government and their own financial liabilities.

They all reached the hotel by the afternoon and parked the Hyundai i10 there. But the Verito containing the weapons was parked in the parking lot of the Jammu and Kashmir Tourism Development Corporation Limited *dak* bungalow on Residency Road. After some time, while

Khalid left with Ashiq to do a recce of the Nagrota Army Camp, the others slept until evening.

'The guard changes between five and six in the morning. That should be the best time for you all to get in,' Ashiq pointed at the camp gate that was guarded by a sentry.

Waiting for a while, Ashiq said, 'I'll drop you here.' He then showed him a spot on the national highway that was at a height. Towards its right, a nullah led into a dense jungle.

Khalid then fished out a map from his bag and asked, 'Is the nullah dry?'

'Yes, and you can walk through it. But there is thick vegetation and you may have to cut some shrubs and branches in order to get to the wall that encircles the cantonment. The wall is not very high,' Ashiq explained.

After Ashiq had acquainted Khalid with the place, they returned to the hotel.

* * *

At around six that evening, Khalid removed a paper slip from his bag and handed it over to Ashiq saying, 'Bhaijaan, we'll need these medicines.'

Ashiq went to a medical store near Gujjar Nagar area and procured the medicines with some injections and syringes. At around seven in the evening, without much interaction with each other, they set course for the Nagrota Army Camp.

Khalid, Numan and Aadil got off 500 metres before the army camp. Khalid removed two pistols from his bag and handed them over to Ashiq as a reward for safely getting them to the attack site and said, 'Khuda Hafiz.'

After exchanging goodbyes, the trio covered their heads with green bands stamped with 'Afzal Guru Squad' and walked stealthily towards the nullah. In the blink of an eye, they vanished into the darkness of the night—the sort of darkness that swallows light and their destiny, which they certainly knew.

Chapter 3

There's a Divinity That Shapes Our Ends

Was it a quirk of fate that Shalini, who was to board a train from Nagrota to Delhi on the 28th, cancelled her booking? On maternity leave, she was not even remotely expected to be there. In fact, Shalini would have been with her husband in Delhi that day: 29 November 2016. Be that as it may . . .

> *'There's a divinity that shapes our ends,*
> *Rough-hew them how we will.'*
Hamlet to Horatio, William Shakespeare.

***

The recession of 2008 had dealt a body blow to many professionals and students who were working hard to shape their careers. Shalini, at the time, had not known that the massive de-leveraging of US banks was going to get her into the Indian Army. Professionals were being handed pink slips and students, despite making it through campus recruitments, were not sure if they would get permanent job offers. Shalini, like many others who could not afford to pursue higher studies abroad, started looking for greener pastures in secure government jobs. She, along with her batchmates applied for government jobs—the army being one of the options. To her surprise, she made it through in the first attempt. Her parents, who thought that the army was all about borders, were nonetheless proud of her achievement. Shalini's siblings too were very happy for her.

* * *

After serving in the army for about six years in remote places, Shalini's parents had their hearts set on seeing their daughter married quickly. As she neither had the time nor a boyfriend, it was left for her parents to do the honours. They found a suitable match for her in Amit Mall—a scientist working with the Defence Research and Development Organization (DRDO). Shalini wholeheartedly accepted her parents' decision as she was completely confident of their wisdom in making the choice. The wedding was solemnized according to Hindu customs, both families being Brahmins. Before her marriage, Shalini had already served as an officer in the Indian Army Corps of Electronics and Mechanical Engineers (EME) in Assam, Baroda and Secunderabad, and was presently posted at Agra. With her marriage to Amit, a well-settled central government employee, her parents were content as life seemed promising for their daughter.

* * *

Like all newly-wed couples, Shalini and Amit were undecided about their honeymoon destination. Amit had to consider accessibility, affordability and aesthetics and finally he booked a holiday in Pokhara, Nepal. Pokhara was close to Gorakhpur, Amit's hometown, and known for its beauty.

'Why not Kathmandu?' Shalini asked.

'Kathmandu is clichéd. Trust me. You won't regret going to Pokhara. I've done my research and know it is way better than Kathmandu. It'll take your breath away.' Amit had put the proposal so well that Shalini had no reason to refuse.

They decided to drive down to Pokhara as the route was very picturesque. Shalini had seen such beauty only in movies, though she had been posted to scenic places like Assam. But this region was quite different and had a charm of its own. They reached Pokhara in the evening of 24 April 2015 and checked into the hotel. After driving about eight hours, they were dead tired and slept like logs. For a newly-wed couple, getting up early in the morning is quite a challenge as it impedes getting to know each other physically and mentally. Amit and Shalini undertook that voyage to be one, but without compromising on their sightseeing plans.

* * *

Shalini laid out a choice of outfits and asked Amit to choose one. She wanted to wear something that her husband would like to see her in. Amit liked them all and just couldn't pick a favourite. Finally, he asked her to wear whatever she wanted, setting the tone for the pace of their married life. *'Jo tumko ho pasand, woh hi baat kahenge* (I'll only say what you love to hear).

'At least pick your favourite colour!' Shalini pleaded. Amit had another look at the dresses and picked up one in red. Red—the colour of life, love, joy and passion. They got ready and after breakfast at the hotel, went to see Mahendra Cave, one of the most famous tourist attractions in Pokhara. Being staunch Hindus, Shalini and Amit wished to begin their journey into married life seeking Lord Shiva's blessings. There was a Shiva idol in the cave. Just as they were about to enter the cave, Shalini suddenly felt the ground under her feet tremble. These were the tremors of one of the most devastating earthquakes that Nepal had ever witnessed. Shalini counted the tremors— one, two, three . . . thirty-nine, forty. In panic, people were jostling each other trying to leave the cave. Amit firmly held Shalini's hand in his and led her in the opposite direction— into the cave.

Shalini was hesitant and asked, 'I just felt several tremors, Amit. Don't you think it's risky to go inside the cave?'

But a calm and confident Amit exhorted, 'We've come so far. Let's not leave without paying obeisance to Lord Shiva. Nothing can happen to us in His shelter.'

Shalini held her husband's hand and they entered the cave. After offering their prayers, they left the cave and returned safely to their hotel. On the way back, they witnessed the unprecedented devastation the earthquake had caused. The hotel staff moved them from the ninth floor to the first for their safety and they stayed for two more days before returning to Gorakhpur. The earthquake played spoilsport, cutting short their remarkably eventful honeymoon. How could they turn a blind eye to the destruction all around?

* * *

It is an accepted fact that most Indian families aim to expand and that too quickly. When Shalini was married in 2015, she was already twenty-eight and there was parental pressure from the couple's families to have a baby. Shalini, like so many other working women, was confused. She had her career on the one hand and the family on the other. She was a woman first, an army officer later. Her maternal instincts kicked in and she decided to give it a serious try. After their wedding, Shalini found herself in Agra while Amit was in Delhi. He would visit her on weekends. But they were not sure if there was enough time for them to seriously think of a baby.

* * *

Shalini was slowly setting up her house. Though she had bought all the household necessities, she missed having a car. The couple then made one of the most important decisions of their lives—the car model. Keeping all major factors in mind—mileage, lucky colour, features, servicing cost, etc., they decided to buy a Maruti Swift Dzire.

* * *

Time has wings and Shalini had barely adjusted to the idea of her husband visiting on the weekends, when she got her posting order to Nagrota, a town located in Jammu district of J&K. It was her first semi-field posting as an army officer. Though she wanted to spend some more time with her husband, just like any other newly-married girl, her career did not allow it. On the other hand, travelling to and fro between Delhi and Nagrota was extremely tiring for Amit.

'How will we ever manage?' Shalini looked at Amit while packing her things in a large number of bags. Though it was an emotionally overwhelming moment for both of them, Amit reassured her saying, 'Don't worry, love, everything will soon be fine.'

Shalini took a deep breath, comforted by her husband's loving words. She tried to forget her insecurities for a while and decided to make their last night together in Agra an unforgettable romantic memory. All through the night, she slept in her husband's arms who took her to dizzying heights of bliss.

* * *

With hope in her heart, she left for Nagrota the following day. She stayed in a guest room for a few days and was later shifted to a temporary accommodation that had a small living room and a bedroom. The process of shifting and settling down in a new place kept Shalini so busy for a month that she almost forgot she had missed her period.

After a week with no sign of her period, she spoke to Amit.

'Why don't you get a pregnancy kit?' he advised Shalini, who hadn't even thought about it. She took her husband's advice seriously when she recalled their moments of unbridled passion in Agra. They had thrown caution to the winds to have a baby. Shalini then reflected that she had indeed been feeling tired with occasional bouts of nausea. Her breasts felt tender as well. And all of a sudden, she realized that night in Agra was just four or five days after her last period. Holding her breath, she did the pregnancy test. Two red lines confirmed her pregnancy. The army had taught her that nothing in life is ever promised and guaranteed, so she wanted proper confirmation of this. She immediately called Amit, letting the reality of finally being pregnant sink in. In a tone barely hiding her excitement, she yelled: '*Jaan*, I think I'm pregnant!'

'What?' Amit was euphoric.

'Yes, there are two lines on the stick!'

'Oh my god! I'm so happy for us. Let me call my family.'

Amit was eager to broadcast his virility before his family, but Shalini threw a spanner in the works.

'Be patient, my love. Let me go to the hospital and get a blood test. I want to be doubly sure before we make it public.'

The army had trained her to be overcautious about everything. Amit agreed. The blood test confirmed Shalini's pregnancy.

* * *

That day, Shalini felt different. She didn't feel alone any more. She was carrying a part of Amit inside her. All her insecurities of being away from Amit disappeared and she suddenly felt more at ease with the long-distance marriage. After knowing how happy Amit was with the news, she thought of everything to keep the 'little Amit' happy and well-fed inside her. She suddenly wanted to eat healthy and live healthy. Amit would not be around—the entire responsibility of the baby was completely on her. She didn't want to let herself, Amit, or their relationship down.

* * *

One evening, after having a sumptuous meal at the mess, Shalini headed back home to sleep early. She changed into comfortable clothes after taking off her uniform. Suddenly, she heard a hissing sound but couldn't figure out where it was coming from. She looked around, turning slowly in the same spot, but the sound disappeared.

Shalini went around the house to locate the source of the sound, but with little success. Passing by her dressing table she caught a fleeting glance of herself in the mirror. Moving closer to the mirror, she stood before it to look at herself. She picked up a comb and started pulling her hair into a ponytail. She then lifted her shirt to look at her belly, something she had been doing quite often. Moving her hand around her belly gently, she wondered when and how it would grow, trying to guess if it would be a boy or a girl. With these thoughts, she lay on her bed and went to sleep. In the few moments before falling asleep, she heard the hissing once again but dismissed it, thinking it was her pregnancy making her hear strange noises. She got into bed and closed her eyes, but from that night onward, sleep often eluded her.

* * *

Shalini continued with her routine but with a few changes: going to the office, taking vitamins and dietary supplements prescribed by the doctor, calling up Amit and imagining that the persistent hissing was the result of hormonal changes due to her pregnancy. She was afraid she would be judged if she told someone she was scared of a hissing sound in her house.

But one day when the hissing was too loud to be ignored, she finally told Amit about it.

'A hissing sound? Could it be a snake?' Amit exclaimed.

'I'm not sure!' Shalini suddenly felt frightened.

'Don't be afraid. Go and get some help,' Amit advised as he was now doubly concerned; for his wife and for their unborn baby.

Shalini went down to the first floor and told the officer living there about the hissing sound.

'I think it's a snake,' she said.

'How can a snake come up to the second floor, ma'am? I don't think that is possible.'

'Let me come up and have a look,' the officer said after seeing how worried Shalini was.

They went upstairs and were greeted by pin-drop silence. The officer looked around the house but couldn't find anything. Shalini was embarrassed but she was sure that there was something in her flat that ought not to be there.

'I don't see anything, ma'am, but in case you face any problem at any time, feel free to call me,' the officer reassured her and left.

The moment he was gone and Shalini was locking her door, there was that hiss again. But she was too tired and embarrassed to call the officer again. She was by now convinced that it was nothing but her pregnancy that was making her imagine such sounds.

***

The mystery of the hissing was finally solved when she came home the next day after dinner. As she unlocked her door and walked in, there in the middle of her living area, was a cobra coiled gracefully. Shalini almost chuckled in relief! All the while she had been blaming her hormones. She stood still without disturbing it. The fear of the unknown is always greater than the fear of the known. She was now less frightened as she knew who her enemy was. And she had been literally sleeping with it in her room for the past one month. She closed the door and let the cobra enjoy its leisure time on her carpet until she called for some help. As she left, she saw it begin to do what could have been called a dance. The army always gives you the most interesting experiences.

The officer on the first floor assumed that it had come inside one of Shalini's crates.

***

That night she was shifted into a guest room. Her accommodation was subjected to a thorough combing operation to find any other snake after they had caught the one found on her carpet. The men who caught the snake from her room believed that cobras often live in pairs. Even after 'operation snake eviction', Shalini insisted that she be shifted elsewhere.

* * *

A few days earlier, Shalini heard that her sister had got engaged. She applied for annual leave and left for Varanasi on 15 October to be with her family and celebrate Diwali with them. Her parents were delighted to see her, more so as they were soon going to be grandparents.

After enjoying her holidays and cocooned in the love and warmth of her parents, Shalini returned to Nagrota on 25 November. She had to get an ultrasound done as part of her regular medical examination before she could go on maternity leave to be with her husband in Delhi. Presently, she was living in her second temporary accommodation with her bags still packed. Since permanent accommodation was not available to her for at least six months, she did not bother to unpack her stuff and left most of it in a military garage along with her car.

* * *

When she went for her appointment with the doctor the next day, she found that the Nagrota Military Hospital did not have an ultrasound facility and she was referred to the Jammu Military Hospital.

Shalini got an appointment for the morning of 27 November and decided to drive down. But the car battery was dead and she had to get it recharged. So, she left the following day and drove all the way to Jammu only to find that the doctor was away on an emergency and her appointment had been cancelled. Shalini's train tickets for Delhi were booked for 28 November. She had to renew the booking for the 29th. The next day, when she was finally able to get her ultrasound done, she was relieved to know that the baby was fine and so was she. She returned from Jammu happy and had a relaxed evening, eagerly looking forward to being in Delhi with her loving husband the next day.

* * *

As usual, she had dinner at eight in the evening and lay in bed. This new place was far from her office and located right in the middle of a jungle. There was dense undergrowth and trees around the place. A large number of shepherds and people from the villages nearby would wander outside the boundary wall and gather wood for their houses while the sheep grazed on the foliage.

Shalini would often hear the sound of axes cutting wood. She was not pleased with civilians being so close to the cantonment wall, but consoled herself that they were probably poor people who were dependent on firewood to cook their food.

There was an uncovered AC vent in the new house that made the sound of branches being cut even more irritating. Shalini did not want to buy an AC to cover the vent as winter was setting in and her stay was temporary. With all these thoughts in her mind, she tried to sleep but could not, possibly due to her advancing pregnancy.

* * *

Around four-thirty in the morning. Shalini was rudely awakened by the sounds of distant gunshots. On regaining her composure, she heard the gunshots get closer. Unlike on previous occasions, she could not blame her pregnancy as the shots sounded far more real than the hiss of the cobra.

More so, her army experience had taught her to recognize that it was not the usual firing training. She wondered if it was a terrorist attack.

Suddenly, there was a loud blast, and she knew then that it was a grenade. Running outside to check, she saw light flashes behind her building that confirmed her doubts.

She ran back inside and called her adjutant to tell him that a terrorist attack was underway. He reassured her, saying that it could have been just firing practice. Shalini insisted that it wasn't and stated, 'I can hear the gunshots right outside my house.' And then there was another blast that the adjutant heard over the phone as well.

***

A catastrophic earthquake on her honeymoon, living in a room with a hissing cobra for a month and now a terrorist attack—Shalini didn't have to go looking for adventures in her life. They seemed to come looking for her!

Though she had survived the disastrous earthquake in Pokhara and then that dreaded cobra in her room, she became suddenly unsure if she would survive the terrorist attack—especially with a baby growing in her womb.

Chapter 4

Will You Marry Me?

Maj. Vinod was fast asleep on the morning of 29 November 2016 and had put his alarm on snooze. It was quite chilly and he was reluctant to leave the warmth of his blankets. His wife Bhanupriya and daughter Shreyasi, who was just over a year old, were sleeping with him until they were all woken up by the sound of gunshots. It would have been a usual day at the office for him had evil not stormed into the cantonment.

***

Vinod hailed from a middle-class background—his father had served in the Indian Air Force and his mother was a homemaker. Like any other student who scored well in the matriculation examination, he too opted for science. He wanted to be a computer engineer, not only because the profession was considered sophisticated, but also because he was genuinely interested in it. Even as a child, Vinod was ambitious and wanted to give his best to the world.

Male students in India who give a serious thought to engineering also consider the National Defence Academy (NDA). Most engineering aspirants appear for the NDA exam as well, and so did Vinod. The UPSC is smarter in many ways. It conducts and declares the results before the National Testing Agency or CBSE does, so that the candidates who clear the NDA exam generally choose to stay put. A bird in hand is worth two in the bush, and it was with that logic that Vinod's parents convinced him to join the NDA. So, even before his engineering entrance tests were conducted, he was making the rounds of the grounds at the NDA campus.

* * *

But, determined to pursue computer engineering, he opted for the same course at the NDA. He didn't know that he would get his degree not just by learning about computers but also by jumping, pumping iron and running in the field. Consequently, at the end of three years in the NDA, Vinod knew more about running 2.5 kilometres in less than nine minutes, doing thirty to thirty-five push-ups and fifteen chin-ups in one go, swimming 1 kilometre in every possible stroke, and climbing a 3-metre rope without using one's legs.

* * *

After the three years in the NDA, he spent another year in the Indian Military Academy (IMA). He got commissioned in an artillery unit in 2005, which was primarily a Khalsa unit posted in Meerut. Most recruits were Sikhs in that unit. He alighted from the train and two Khalsa jawans picked him up. They took his luggage and drove Vinod to his unit in a Gypsy. He was then taken to a ground where a football match was being played. A senior officer who was watching the match looked at him and asked him if he knew how to play football. Vinod answered that he did.

'Leave your bag, change into your sports gear and join the match,' commanded the officer. Vinod doubled up and played well.

Only after he had proved his worth on the field, did the senior officer ask him who he was.

He was inducted into the unit with that brief about himself and asked to live in the barracks with the jawans to know his men better. Being a Bihari, the biggest challenge that Vinod faced was remembering the faces of the Khalsas. For him, they all looked alike. Another challenge he faced was remembering their unisex names. He would call out 'Gurpreet!' and there would be five reporting in. But within a few months, he not only knew every jawan of his unit by their face and name but also their strengths, weaknesses, hometowns and in some cases, their family members as well.

***

After Meerut, Vinod's unit was posted to the Siachen glacier. Vinod had only heard, but never experienced what a temperature difference of 100 degrees would feel like: plus 40 in Meerut to minus 40 there. Vinod realized this difference when his morning tea would freeze if he snoozed for a few minutes after his buddy woke him up with a cuppa.

The pressure was so low there that cooking in a pressure cooker was fruitless, so they would have to smash the potatoes and tomatoes before they could boil them. Low oxygen levels kept them from eating more and hence, weight loss amongst soldiers was a common phenomenon. The endurance limit of Vinod's body was tested in the freezing conditions.

* * *

With the advent of winter, the temperature was falling at Vinod's post and the last temperature that he recorded with the help of an alcohol thermometer was minus 45 degrees. After three months, he went on leave to his hometown, Patna. When he shaved for the first time in three months, he realized that he had lost 14 kilos. Experts told him that low pressure and low oxygen levels at the glacier kept him from eating, which resulted in the generation of energy from fat. And when the fat stored in his body was over, his body began breaking down muscles. During that leave, he made up for it by relishing the food that his mother cooked for him. He wasn't sure when he would get to savour it next.

When Vinod returned to his post, he saw the thermometer still showing a temperature of minus 45 degrees whereas in reality, the temperature was much lower than that. The last reading that an alcohol thermometer could give was minus 45. For the rest of the tenure, Vinod and his men continued to smash the potatoes and tomatoes, and survived the conditions successfully.

* * *

After gaining more military experience in Siachen, Vinod was posted as an instructor in the Officers Training Academy (OTA) and with this, he revisited his own academy days.

A lot of cadets are clueless about what arm to join after their training and most instructors would proudly call out their own arms and units. But Vinod always advised them to join what they wanted. Like choosing a girl for marriage was a personal choice, so was choosing the arm that a soldier was going to be serving in for the rest of his life until he retired. And that advice helped many cadets pursue their passion.

***

Just as Vinod was giving this advice to the cadets in the academy, his mother was conspiring to get him married. Before he came to Patna on leave, he had already spoken to three girls but couldn't find his match in them. He wanted to choose a girl like he had chosen his arm in the Indian Army—something that he cared for from the depths of his heart and that would keep him happy and content for the rest of his life.

When Vinod reached Patna, his parents had already arranged for a meeting with Bhanupriya and her family. Bhanupriya was a simple girl. When Vinod saw her, he fell in love with her simplicity. She was dressed in a simple saree with just a little kohl in her eyes. They met in a restaurant at the Patna Zoo. A part of the zoo, the restaurant was very popular and the parents, much to the amusement of their children, thought it to be an ideal place for a discussion on a prospective matrimonial alliance.

* * *

Poets have coined the phrase 'love at first sight' very aptly, and Vinod and Bhanupriya reaffirmed it. Vinod decided that he wanted to marry Bhanupriya and the rest was just a formality. When his parents asked him to talk to her alone, he decided to take a stroll with her around the zoo.

Vinod led Bhanupriya towards the walkthrough that took them towards the zoo. They walked for a while without uttering a word to each other. Vinod tried to steal a glance at Bhanupriya as they walked side by side. The small silver *jhumkas* in her ears, the loose strands of hair flying around in the breeze and the small droplets of sweat trickling down from her neck made Vinod wonder how a girl of her simplicity could look so beautiful. He quickly turned away when Bhanupriya looked up at him. He did not want her to think he was a lech.

Now, instead of focusing on her, he was looking at the chimpanzees and monkeys in the zoo. He wondered how the human race had evolved from them, yet behaved no differently—life's basic instincts are so deeply ingrained that sophistication fails to camouflage them. After walking a little more, Vinod realized that he had left Bhanupriya behind. It was apparent that she was finding it rather difficult to catch up with Vinod in a saree and chappals. Vinod immediately turned around to be with her.

'Are you all right?' Vinod asked her. She just nodded without uttering a word.

'I'm fine. It's just that you walk very fast,' Bhanupriya said, smiling.

'Damn NDA training!' Vinod exclaimed, smiling back.

* * *

The NDA training prepares you for many things, but walking in a zoo with a girl you want to marry was just not one of them, thought Vinod.

He slowed down to match his pace to his future life partner. And that's what they were going to do for the rest of their lives after tying the nuptial knot.

After a while, Vinod summoned all his courage, far more than that required to pass the PT test, and proposed, 'Will you marry me?'

Bhanupriya blushed, nodded to convey her acceptance and then meekly asked, 'Can I study after marriage?'

Vinod who did not know how to respond to such an innocent question, quipped, 'You can do whatever you want. You don't need my permission for it.'

Though Vinod would have never stopped Bhanupriya from doing what she wanted to, he was happy that she had asked him—it somehow made him feel important.

'What do you want to study?'

'I'm doing a diploma in textile engineering. I think I can make a career out of it.' Bhanupriya seemed to be really interested in the course.

Vinod, having seen the functioning of the army, wasn't very confident that Bhanupriya would ever have a career in textile engineering, but he was sure that he would give her so much love that she would have no regrets about marrying him.

'Why don't you pursue a BEd degree? Most army officers' wives do it thinking that there will always be a school in an army station. You can have a career as a teacher like your parents.' Vinod was practical, but it was only a suggestion and he left it to Bhanupriya to take the final call.

She shifted the focus on Vinod and asked him, 'What have you studied?'

'I've done ten plus two minus three,' Vinod sounded funny.

'What?' she was shocked. And after a pause, asked, 'What do you mean?'

'I joined the NDA after ten plus two,' Vinod replied and reminisced about his NDA days. His induction, training and passing out flashed before his eyes. He shook his head and returned to the beautiful reality of a gorgeous girl walking beside him whom he wanted to marry.

'Though I had opted for computer science as a subject, I'm not sure if I ended up learning it.' Vinod didn't want to talk much about warfare, thinking she wouldn't understand it and it would scare her.

They were engaged the very next day and married within a few months. It was in 2010, when Vinod was posted as an instructor in the Officers Training Academy (OTA), that Bhanupriya joined him in Chennai. Bhanupriya enjoyed the metro culture of the city, though she took time to get acclimatized to its weather. On most evenings, like any other newly-wed couple, they would be out strolling and tasting the array of street food.

Bhanupriya had just adjusted to the vibe and culture of the OTA, when she heard that they would be shifting to Assam as Vinod had been posted to Assam Rifles. While Vinod was very neutral to the news, Bhanupriya was a little overwhelmed. Vinod had signed up for this uncertainty when he had joined the Indian Army and Bhanupriya too, by default, when she married him.

They both packed their belongings in conventional wooden boxes that were painted black with Vinod's full name written on them along with his rank.

* * *

The Assam Rifles is the only paramilitary force with a dual control structure. While the administrative control of the force is with the Ministry of Home Affairs (MHA), its operational control is with the Indian Army under the Ministry of Defence (MoD). This means that salaries and infrastructure for the force is provided by the MHA, but the deployment, posting, transfer and deputation of the personnel is decided by the army. All its senior ranks, from DG to IG and sector headquarters are manned by officers from the army.

Vinod didn't know that he was going to learn the most important aspects of military operations in those four years in Assam Rifles.

During the fourteen-day orientation programme in Assam Rifles, he underwent live training where different situations were created for the soldiers. For instance, they had to overcome obstacles in a simulated war or terrorist attack. He was exposed to case studies of past operations and received an overview of insurgency in that area. It was a great learning period for him.

* * *

Vinod was still posted in Assam Rifles when he was the presiding officer for a case in one of the units. An officer was fired at by a militant in the adjoining area where Vinod was posted. That officer got hit on his forearm. Surprised it wasn't a direct shot, the officer had ducked inside his barracks. When the militant's bullets got over and he was changing the magazine of his gun, the officer stood up and tried to gauge the situation from the window. It was then the militant took a shot again. The officer did not get hit by a direct bullet but one that ricocheted off a grill and hit his forearm. During the investigation Vinod grasped that not only should you avoid getting hit by a direct bullet, but also by a ricochet.

* * *

Vinod's next posting was in Nagrota where he joined his unit. He was very happy about being back with his unit officers as that was home-away-from-home for him.

Chapter 5

Mumli

Maj. Ajay had left for office in the early hours of 29 November 2016 without waking his wife Meenu who had slept late that night. Amayra, their eight-month-old daughter, had been cranky all through the night and he did not feel like disturbing them. Quietly, he put on his uniform, looked lovingly back at his wife and daughter, before gently closing the door shut without latching it.

**

It was an ordinary day for Meenu. She had just returned from college and was extremely hungry. Meenu lived with her parents in Bhiwani. She was a BTech and was pursuing her MTech, while working part-time as an assistant professor in an engineering college.

Meenu always dreamt of joining the Indian Army and then marrying an army officer. Coming from a conservative Rajput family, she was often advised to continue with teaching as that was considered the most suitable profession for girls marrying army officers.

* * *

Tired of her MTech studies, followed by the lectures she had to deliver, she wearily put her bag in her cupboard and called her mother, 'Mumli, how about lunch? I'm damn hungry.' She lovingly used the nickname for her mom, Mumli. Her mother had been eagerly waiting for her to reach home and look at the photograph of a prospective match. She beckoned Meenu close and handed her the photograph of a smart young man in Indian Air Force uniform.

'Lunch can wait, *beta*, first have a look at this.'

Meenu sneered at the picture saying, 'So dusky? I won't marry him, Mumli.'

Meenu's mother looked at her daughter with disgust and admonished, 'How can you judge someone by the colour of his skin? You're the only girl from our village who is so well educated and yet you have such a regressive outlook.'

'Mumli, I have my Service Selection Board (SSB) interview coming up in less than three weeks' time. You'll be proud of me. I'll be an officer. So, don't lure me with these marriage proposals. I'm not ready yet, you know that. Can I please have lunch now? I'm dying of hunger,' Meenu cajoled her mother.

* * *

Meenu's father, who was listening to the banter between his wife and daughter from the other room said, '*Arrey*, she is hungry. Why don't you give her food first and discuss everything else later?'

Meenu's father, like most fathers, always came to his daughter's rescue. He was her true friend. From getting her the latest mobile phone to rejecting boys for a matrimonial alliance, he was Meenu's partner in crime. He would leave no stone unturned for his daughter's happiness. Once he bought her one of the most expensive mobile phones in the market, but asked the mobile store to give him a bill of a lower amount. It would spare them Meenu's mother's ire!

'Papa! Look at this photo. Just look at it! Ma wants me to get married to this man!'

Meenu handed over the photo to her father while her mother made her way to the kitchen.

'This is what happens when our daughters are educated beyond a certain level. They lose their minds,' Meenu's mother blurted angrily while placing Meenu's lunch on the table.

'Give me something to eat as well.' Meenu's father was tempted looking at the bowl of freshly-made okra.

'But you just had your lunch!' Meenu's mother exclaimed. She took special care of her husband's food and health after he had suffered a heart attack about fifteen years ago.

'So what! I'll have a small bite with my daughter.'

'I'm fed up of being in the kitchen the whole day. And on top of that, there is no electricity. Get a generator or I'll die of a heat-stroke one day. This inverter can't take the load of the air conditioner,' Meenu's mother grumbled while wiping beads of sweat with the *pallu* of her saree.

'Your wish is my command, lady! I'll get it for you,' Meenu's father bowed in mock reverence.

Finding her father in a good mood, Meenu lost no time in asking for a favour. 'Papa, Mumli is not letting me change my earrings. She has locked the new ones in her cupboard.'

'She hasn't given them to you yet? I've asked her to do so weeks ago.'

'No, papa!' Meenu said making her sad-puppy face.

Meenu's father looked up at his wife angrily as she placed a plate of food in front of her husband. He refused to eat it.

'What happened?' Meenu's mother first looked at her husband and then at her daughter. Meenu looked away.

'Hand over those earrings you got from the jeweller to Meenu immediately,' her father ordered.

'She will lose them. She's already lost one pair. They are hers but she will get them only when she gets married,' Meenu's mother argued.

'I'll get her another pair on that occasion. For now, let her have the one in your almirah.'

Meenu's mother went to the bedroom and opened the locker. She took out the earrings and closed the locker after giving a cursory glance at all the jewellery she had purchased with the savings of her husband's hard-earned money.

She walked into the room where her husband and daughter were discussing the imminent SSB interview. Meenu was showing the call letter to her father. Her love for the armed forces was unmatched. After clearing her written exam, she had been called for the SSB interview. She was extremely excited as well as nervous.

Meenu and her father ended their conversation abruptly as they saw Meenu's mother approaching them with the earrings. Meenu grabbed them from her mother and put them on.

Meenu's father looked at his daughter dotingly as she gestured to him for a compliment. He only smiled at her approvingly and she left the room happily as her father started eating.

'You've spoilt her beyond belief. She will have problems when she goes to her in-laws' house,' Meenu's mother said, shaking her head.

'I'm always there to take care of her problems, don't you worry,' Meenu's father assured his wife as he took a bite of his food.

But no matter how many times a man gives assurances, life takes its own course. And life, in a nutshell, is the culmination of happiness and sadness. Soon after, Meenu lost her father to a cardiac arrest; it was the biggest loss of her life to date.

* * *

Meenu didn't attend college the next day. Not finding her friend in college, Sonika called Meenu and was concerned to hear Meenu's quavering voice.

'Papa is no more, Sonika,' Meenu burst into tears.

'What happened? When did this happen? How?' Sonika asked in disbelief.

Meenu patiently explained everything and Sonika promised to meet her at the earliest.

* * *

After a few days, Meenu met Sonika along with a few other friends and all of them offered her their condolences. Most of them knew how attached Meenu had been to her father so they tried to comfort her as much as possible.

'Will you be going for the SSB interview?' Sonika was concerned.

'I don't think so, Sonika,' was Meenu's instant reply.

Sonika didn't want to say anything as in situations like these it is sometimes best to hold your counsel. Sensing her friend's silence, Meenu said, 'Mumli will need me at home and moreover, I don't think I'm in the best state of mind for the interview.'

'But this is your last chance, Meenu!' Sonika reminded her of something that she already knew, but for Meenu it was a conscious decision. So, on 20 July, Meenu didn't appear for the interview and all the dreams she had harboured as a little girl were abandoned.

* * *

After Meenu's father's demise, the family took a while to collect themselves. It was an irreparable loss for each one of them. Sometimes Band-Aids don't work and wounds refuse to heal. It would often happen with Meenu and her family. The only option life gives you is to move on, and gradually, they began to come to terms with the loss.

Meenu's mother was all the more worried for her daughter now. With her husband gone, the whole responsibility of the house was on her shoulders. Meenu was acutely aware of the fact that her mother wanted her to get married as soon as possible. She didn't want to add to her mother's miseries by declining any more proposals.

* * *

Sonika had joined the air force and was in touch with Meenu on social media. One day she called Meenu who didn't know that the call was going to change her life.

'Meenu, I know a boy who wants to get married. You must meet him,' Sonika gushed.

'But why me? Why not you?' Meenu questioned in surprise.

'He says that he can't settle down with a working woman who doesn't wear a saree. And you know me.'

Meenu didn't know whether her friend was happy about the fact that she was an air force officer or sad about the fact that the boy she was recommending didn't want a working wife. Meenu remained silent.

'He is a good guy and I don't want you to let him go. I have a strong hunch that both of you will click. There is no harm meeting him. If you don't like him, you can say no. I'll set up a meeting.' Sonika waited impatiently for her friend's answer.

'Okay, what does he do?' Meenu asked hesitantly.

'Now we are talking. He is in the Indian Army and I've known him for a long time now. He is very tall and handsome. He is a Rajput, so your mom will not have a problem and he is looking to settle down. It's a perfect match.' Sonika was really excited. Doing something for her friend was giving her a different kind of joy. It was a mission of utmost importance to her.

* * *

Ajay had taken leave to meet his parents and they were keen to get him married. Ajay wasn't averse to the idea; it was just that he didn't want to get married to any of the girls chosen by his parents. He respected his parents to such an extent that it appeared to others as if he was scared of them. But Ajay's respect for his parents was not based on fear but on the love they had for him. He realized the importance of bringing a girl into the family who understood their culture and traditions. But at the same time, he wanted someone who was flexible and understood his professional challenges.

* * *

When Meenu told her mother she was going to meet a boy, she was happy and relieved that her daughter was finally thinking about marriage. When you're in your early twenties and exploring life, you may not always know right from wrong. But as you explore life, you allow yourself to drift with the wind in search of your destiny.

Meenu and Ajay seemed to be two such explorers when they met on 16 May 2013 in a restaurant in Bhiwani. Ajay almost kidnapped his cousin who was studying BTech so that he could lend him moral support. He would have never needed that support to shoot the enemy at the border, but the situation at hand seemed more grave and life-changing.

***

Meenu was sitting at a table, waiting for her Prince Charming to arrive. To her surprise, he actually turned out to be one. She instantly found him good-looking. Her heart skipped a beat and she had butterflies in her stomach at the sight of the tall and handsome man who stood in front of her. But she managed to maintain a calm demeanour.

'Hi, I'm Ajay and he is my cousin,' Ajay introduced themselves and grabbed a chair.

'I'm Meenu,' Meenu smiled at him.

'Would you like to have something?' Meenu asked Ajay when the waiter arrived at their table.

'Yes, some water,' Ajay told the waiter.

Ajay finished the entire jug of water that the waiter had placed before him and then asked for more. Watching Ajay drink so much water, Meenu felt guilty for making him travel all the way from Jaipur to Bhiwani.

'Why don't you have a cold drink? It's such a hot day.'

She called the waiter and asked him to bring them cold drinks. Ajay asked for a Coca Cola while Meenu asked for Fanta.

'I know you always have Fanta, ma'am,' the waiter smiled at Meenu, trying to show his familiarity in the hope of a good tip.

'Sugarcane juice is very cheap in your city. On our way we had two glasses of juice each,' Ajay tried to strike up a conversation.

'Yes, just Rs 20 for a big glass,' Meenu said proudly.

Ajay could see that Meenu took pride in small things. She seemed simple and uncomplicated to him. Meenu, meanwhile, was just happy that her city could effectively cater to a stranger's needs.

'Do you always wear a saree?' It was Ajay's first question.

'No, not always. There are occasions when I wear other clothes too. But in our family, the women mostly wear sarees. What about your family?'

'Not just a saree, you'll have to wear a *ghagra choli* and a *ghunghat*. Can you do that?' Ajay was clear.

Meenu had never met a man who was so honest in his demands. He seemed to be very clear about what he wanted.

'Of course! I can do that. But what can you do?' Meenu asked, looking directly into his eyes.

'I can love you, take care of you and keep you happy,' Ajay said confidently.

'I'm not here to waste your and my time,' he continued. 'I've travelled all the way from Jaipur in this scorching heat to let you know that I'm serious about marriage. Let me know what you think because *faujis* are always running short of time. Do you expect anything out of me? Please don't hesitate to tell me.'

Ajay was definitely in a hurry and didn't mince his words.

'What about my career and profession?' Meenu asked.

'I'll be honest, Meenu. I am in a profession where my wife cannot have a profession and I cannot have that beautiful married life that I have always envisioned. I want to know if you can fit into that vision. If you have dreams of pursuing a profession, I'm not the man you should marry. I know girls who have a good professional career and wanted to marry me but I didn't want to cheat them by giving them a false, rosy picture of life with an officer. The life of an army officer is not easy and it's even more difficult for his spouse. We need our spouse to help us stay sane; at least I do. I've been honest with my demands and now you have to make a choice. Do you want to keep me sane?' Ajay gave a winsome smile to Meenu.

Ajay was sure that he had played his hand well and had laid out all his cards, but he couldn't ascertain whether Meenu was convinced.

Meenu was in pursuit of happiness. And here was a man promising not just happiness but much more. To her, his honesty was seductive and the idea of marriage with him appeared promising. She looked down at her fingers as she thought hard. Finally, she looked up at the man who was staring at her anxiously. With all her faith, she smiled and said yes to him. It was a big decision; one that would impact and transform the rest of her life. But she had faith. It's miraculous how some people will face challenges thrown at them with knowledge, but none with faith.

* * *

In the next meeting, Ajay met Meenu's parents and things were soon formalized between the two families. They had a courtship period of about ten months. Ajay would not spare any effort to be in touch with his lady love.

After being posted in the Gurez Valley, Ajay came down to Leh where there were better means of communication and so he was more frequently in touch with Meenu. While speaking on the phone, she could overhear Ajay giving commands to his subordinates as there would be multiple communication channels open: '*Move the trucks from there immediately. The courier has to reach today at any cost!*'

When Meenu would be put on hold, she listened curiously to the cacophony of Ajay's workplace. She kept wondering if he worked in a call centre or in the transport department.

That day, she called up her younger brother. After exchanging niceties, Meenu came straight to the point, 'Pradeep, I hope this guy, Ajay, is an army officer. Listening to him at work, he seems to be a call centre executive!' She paused for a moment and continued, 'Or maybe a transport manager. Why don't you find out for me, please?'

'Are you crazy?' Pradeep exclaimed and burst out laughing. Meenu was relieved. Her brother's laugh was enough to confirm that Ajay was, in fact, an army officer. So what if she could not become an officer herself; she was getting married to one, and she had started loving him.

The calls between Ajay and Meenu continued. They spoke about the birds and the bees and the facts of life. Their love for each other grew over their conversations. Never for a moment did they regret the proposal that had come in one fortunate meeting.

***

One year had gone by since Meenu and Ajay were formally engaged, but Ajay's professional commitments were keeping him from formalizing the relationship. Meenu's family was getting restless. Understanding the impatience and the gravity of the situation, Ajay asked his parents to hasten the formalities. A panditji was consulted for an auspicious date for the wedding—4 July 2013.

Just two years and one day after her father's demise, Meenu was married to Ajay. Meenu wondered why there wasn't an auspicious date before the fourth. Again she couldn't find a reason but believed that her father was still protecting her like a guardian angel from the heavens above. Her faith didn't need a reason.

* * *

Meenu and Ajay began their life together. They were a good match and got along well. In fact, Meenu was having the time of her life with Ajay when she realized she was pregnant— which usually happens when a newly married couple throws caution to the winds. They decided to move ahead with the pregnancy though they were not really prepared for it.

On 26 March 2016, they welcomed their daughter and named her Amayra—a regal and beautiful princess.

* * *

After places like Dinjan and Lalagarh Jattan, Ajay was posted to Nagrota. He joined his new place of posting in September 2016, and immediately went out of town on official work. Having settled Meenu and Amayra in a guest room accommodation near an officers' mess, Ajay left the station. Meenu didn't have many people to interact with there so she went for a walk every day with Amayra and did some shopping.

* * *

When Ajay got back from duty, both Meenu and Amayra were very happy to have him back. Though Nagrota wasn't like any other metropolitan city, Meenu was just happy that she could stay with her husband. Having the family together, though under a tin roof, was all that she had desired. For her, it was no less than heaven on earth.

Chapter 6

From Blue to Olive

Honorary Captain Yogendra Singh Yadav, Param Vir Chakra awardee for his action during the Kargil War, was in Bengaluru in 2017 for a motivational talk. There, he got an opportunity to meet Meghna Girish, the mother of late Maj. Akshay Girish. As a part of the extended military family, he wished to pay his regards to her.

On meeting Meghna, he asked her, 'Ma'am, when did you come to know?'

'It was around half past six in the evening when we received the call,' Meghna replied with a sigh that never seemed to leave her heart.

'But when did *you* know?' Capt. Yogendra asked her again.

And that was the first time Meghna realized that she knew about her son much before everyone else; after all, they had been joined by the umbilical cord for nine months. A mother knows everything about her child all through her life—the child remains an inseparable part of her being even after the birth, through an invisible divine connection.

During Akshay's birth, when the umbilical cord was cut, she had suffered happily as it breathed life into his body. But now she wished that the umbilical cord had never been severed and that she could have kept him cocooned in the safety of her womb for eternity.

* * *

It was a regular morning for Meghna Girish on 29 November 2016. She woke up at around six-thirty in the morning and as was her habit, picked up her phone to check the notifications. Her husband, Wing Commander Girish Kumar, who had served in the Indian Air Force as a Jaguar fighter pilot and was now a commercial pilot after premature retirement, had left home for an early morning flight.

Meghna had been married to Wing Commander Girish for over thirty years. She would fondly remember the years when she had joined Girish in Ambala just after their wedding. Girish was a Jaguar pilot then. While he was thrilled about the fact that he was married to a beautiful woman, inside and out, Girish didn't want to start a family just yet. He thought that they were too young and his profession was rather demanding then. He had requested Meghna to wait a while. From Ambala, Girish was posted to Gorakhpur and Meghna joined him there. But she couldn't spend too much time with him as Girish was busy setting up a new squadron and was mostly away.

There was constant ferrying of aircraft from Hindustan Aeronautics Ltd, Bengaluru, to Gorakhpur. Like his squadron mates, Girish was heavily involved in the process and was neck-deep in work. Meghna decided to join her parents in Bengaluru as she didn't want to be a distraction for Girish while he was doing something so significant. As the new squadron took shape, Girish, while on a work trip to Bengaluru, luckily got to meet his wife at her parents' place. A few days after he left, Meghna started suffering from morning sickness. She was pregnant. Meghna wrote a letter to Girish informing him of her pregnancy. Rather than being excited or shocked, Girish was confused. This hadn't been part of the plan. But Meghna's sheer elation helped Girish make up his mind. He accepted the early pregnancy and brought Meghna back to Gorakhpur.

***

Girish, by then, had started night flying. He would go to the squadron late in the evening and return early in the morning. It was on one of those ordinary mornings when Girish returned early from flying, that Meghna noticed there was something very different about him. He was quiet and seemed preoccupied. She couldn't figure out what it was until he told her that he had lost one of his colleagues in an air crash. He asked Meghna to get ready to go and pay their condolences to the family.

Being an army officer's daughter, Meghna was familiar with this kind of news, but she was new to facing the wife of a pilot lost doing his duty. She accompanied Girish to his colleague's house and from a distance she could hear loud crying—an old woman beating her chest and cursing the dead pilot's wife, 'She ate up our son!'

The poor woman who had just lost her husband was isolated from her husband's family. She who needed to be comforted the most, stood silently, sobbing alone in her immeasurable grief.

Meghna was shocked to see her plight and prayed that no woman should ever have to go through such a tragedy.

* * *

A few days after the death, Meghna was scheduled for her regular pregnancy check-up at the air force hospital in Gorakhpur. The hospital had been set up recently and didn't have enough facilities. They had gynaecologists at the hospital but ultrasound machines and other equipment were missing. Then Meghna developed a random fever that wouldn't leave her for weeks, but none of the doctors could diagnose her ailment. The doctors in Gorakhpur wanted Meghna to be shifted to a bigger and better equipped hospital as the duration of the fever had crossed twenty days. They were not only concerned about the baby but Meghna as well. She was therefore shifted to Command Hospital, Bengaluru, where her parents were present to take care of her. It was there that her fever subsided with aggressive antibiotic injections, but she developed pregnancy-induced hypertension. In the eighth month of her pregnancy, an ultrasound revealed that she was carrying twins.

Meghna loved children and was thrilled to know that she was going to have two of them. Her only concern was Girish. He wasn't ready for one and Meghna was about to gift him two. She wanted to share her happiness with Girish and wrote him a letter:

Dearest Girish,

Today has been a surprise and a shock—I can't wait to share it with you. Daddy took me for a regular check-up and as the doctor was worried about my BP and size of my tummy, he insisted on an ultrasound. I kept saying that my reports must have been mixed up with another lady who has been on fertility treatment. But no—it is me carrying twins! Double Trouble or Twice as Nice: what's your reaction, fighter?

Honestly, this is like a bolt from the blue—I don't think anyone has had twins on either side of the family. Dad kept smiling and said, 'So what—you're the chosen ones. Enjoy the feeling and they will be a blessing to the whole family.'

The doctor insists I need to spend the rest of my pregnancy in hospital because of the hypertension and oedema. There go my plans of a haircut and some decent clothes that fit me! It's going to be bed rest from now on—how I wish you were here. Even a letter takes so long to reach, Saabji.

***

When Girish received the letter from his wife, he excitedly tore it open. His jaw dropped and he stood there with his mouth open.

'What happened?' Girish's flight commander asked, looking at him curiously.

'We're having twins!' Girish exclaimed and the whole squadron cheered and rejoiced at the news.

Girish reached a day after Meghna prematurely delivered two babies via C-section a month before the due date—a boy and a girl. They were named Akshay and Neha.

* * *

As a new mother, and of twins at that, Meghna was realizing many things. And one of them was that it certainly wasn't easy to be a mother to twins. Though she had some help from the nurses in the hospital, she was finding it extremely difficult to manage them both. After a few days, she was discharged. Thankfully, she had enough help from her mother and mother-in-law. On the eleventh day, the babies were taken to a Ganesha temple for blessings in keeping with the family tradition.

Since Neha and Akshay were low-birth weight and high-risk babies, they hadn't developed the reflex action to suckle. As a result, they had to be force-fed by the doctors and were very weak, Akshay being weaker than Neha.

Even after a month, Akshay wasn't putting on any weight nor crying and it was worrying Meghna no end. When they went to a paediatrician, instead of the assurance they were expecting, he scared them to such an extent that Meghna burst into tears at the thought of losing Akshay. Until the time she did not have Akshay, she never knew the fear of losing him. She consoled herself that at least he was right there in her arms, though frail and weak, and fighting to survive.

At that moment, looking at his small face, Meghna decided that no matter what the doctor said, she would pray, care and fight for her baby. She would give it her all to make sure he lived. She was determined that she would not lose her son. Meghna's mother vowed to pay a visit to the Tirupati temple with her family to seek blessings for Akshay's well-being.

Meghna decided to consult another paediatrician. The doctor stripped Akshay naked and the baby wailed on the examination table. Meghna couldn't bear to see her baby crying and put her hand on his barely-developed chest to pacify him.

'Let him cry, ma'am,' the doctor insisted. 'He has to cry to expand his lungs. You're actually doing him a favour if you're letting your baby cry.'

After a few minutes of letting Akshay cry, the doctor asked Meghna to feed him. Akshay thirstily gulped down half a bottle of milk. Meghna had tears of gratitude watching him sleep with his tummy full.

After talking to the new paediatrician who told Meghna to never compare two babies, Meghna realized that there was no fixed way of bringing up children. She bought the book *Dr Benjamin Spock's Baby and Childcare* from a nearby bookstore, and that became her Bible while bringing up her twins.

* * *

Being an air force pilot, Girish, though posted in Gorakhpur, continued to be out on temporary duties besides the three-month-long Pilot Attack Instructors course. Meghna had been away from him for a long time, and she decided to join Girish when the twins were six months old. She also knew, no matter how much her parents and in-laws were willing to assist in bringing up her twins, she would have to ultimately do it herself with the support of their father.

From Gorakhpur they moved to Chennai for Girish's Flying Instructors Course, followed by a posting to Bidar where Neha and Akshay started kindergarten before they turned three. Meghna resumed work, teaching at a pharmacy college. After Bidar, Girish got selected for the prestigious staff college course and they moved to Wellington.

During that period, Neha and Akshay, barely four, were happy exploring a new place, making friends and enjoying a new school. Girish did very well, balancing a highly demanding course with taking the twins for pony rides and treks. For the rest of the time, Meghna was always at their disposal. After being awarded the Lentaigne Medal of the course, Girish moved back to his squadron in Gorakhpur for a short while and then got posted as an instructor to the Air Force Station in Tambaran, Chennai.

* * *

By now the twins were in Class IV. While Neha was a quiet child, Akshay was just the opposite. He was outgoing and always stood up for the right thing. For instance, he never bullied anyone and he refused to be bullied either. But there were some senior boys in his school who disliked

Akshay's attitude. No matter how much those boys tormented him, Akshay was never undignified. He not only believed in winning but also in fighting fair.

One day Meghna found Akshay and Neha walking back home, buddy-hugging each other. They looked dishevelled and as they came closer, Meghna realized that Akshay's shirt was torn, the buttons of Neha's shirt were missing and their shirts were hanging out.

'What happened?' Meghna asked, holding Akshay by the arm. Akshay remained quiet but Neha spoke up, 'Ma, we had a fight.'

'Fight? But I just saw you walking in, hugging each other. When did you two fight?' Meghna was confused.

'No, ma! Not us. There were four boys beating Akshay, so I had to save him!' Neha was triumphant.

'Why did you have to step in?' Meghna knew Neha was a calm but strong girl.

'I had to protect my brother, ma. They can't beat him up like that!' she said excitedly, while trying to make her mother understand something as basic as being by her brother's side.

'Who was beating him?' Meghna wanted to know.

'There were five boys from a senior class,' Neha told her mother.

'Why were they beating him? Did he do something to them?'

Meghna was more concerned about the reason for the fight.

'No, ma!' an exasperated Neha was finding it difficult to describe the incident to her mother.

Seeing that Neha wasn't able to explain things clearly, Akshay stepped in, 'I was the one who had a fight with them, ma . . .'

This was the least he could have done for his sister who had just saved him from being beaten black and blue.

'So, Neha helped me.'

Meghna was hugely amused by her munchkins, knowing that it was the turning point in the relationship between the siblings. It was a point where Neha and Akshay were subconsciously accepting their biological bonding, which was imperatively propelling them to nurture the newfound love between them. It was comforting to see them standing up for each other. They'd always have each other's backs, she was certain.

* * *

One day, a male teacher made a very lewd and sexist remark saying that girls' skirts were getting shorter by the day. While all the other boys laughed, Akshay got up from his seat and told the teacher, 'Sir, this is not right. You can't speak like that about girls.'

While the teacher fumed, Neha observed the reaction of other students and was pleasantly surprised to see her classmates look at her brother with respect. Her chest swelled with pride. Once they were home, she narrated the incident to their mother with delight.

Akshay reluctantly told his mother that the same teacher had summoned her because he was 'being impertinent'. Meghna smiled at him. She wanted to reassure her son and exhorted, 'I'm glad you stood up for the right thing. When you do, you don't have to worry about anything.' Meghna saw her son's glum face turn happy.

* * *

Children owe a lot to their parents for what they become. Meghna wanted her children to have the assurance of her continued support. She wanted them to have the courage to stand for what they believed in. She was proud of her son and knowing he was right, was ready to defend him at any cost. Akshay was also a caring and expressive son. Even though he was so young, when Meghna returned home after a long day at college, he would head straight to the kitchen and bring her a glass of water. He insisted she rest a few moments before beginning her chores. The mother-son bond was becoming more special each passing day.

* * *

Tough times were to follow, though. Meghna lost her sister-in-law to a snake bite. It was a very difficult time for the family and they were needed to help her brother and parents cope with the tragedy. So they decided to shift to Bengaluru. Responsibilities are never given but taken, and Meghna assumed the responsibility of being around her young, motherless nephews.

Dhruv was just thirteen days older than Neha and Akshay, while Satwik was only three. Neha, Akshay and Dhruv grew up as triplets together in Bengaluru and went to the same school. Satwik, meanwhile, had just begun kindergarten. Akshay wanted to join the Military School, Bengaluru after Class V but Meghna felt he was too young and only let him appear for the entrance test after he completed Class VII. Akshay prepared well and sailed through the test. Over the next five years, he became a 'proud Georgian', a boarder in the military school. Although he wasn't allowed home even on the weekends, Meghna would ride her Kinetic Honda to meet Akshay whenever she could, often with Neha and their pet dog, Teeny. She'd meet his friends and they loved the homemade dishes she would take along for them.

* * *

School vacations were times of travel, adventure and bonding for the family. On one such break from school, they explored parts of Uttarakhand. While trekking up from Govindghat to Ghangariya on the way to Hemkund Sahib, a fight broke out between criminals and the police, just as Meghna, Girish and the twins reached their lodge for the night. As the sounds of fighting, bullets and screams grew louder, the terrified chowkidar barely managed to hand over the keys to their rooms before running away, warning the family to lock themselves up and not step out. Girish and Neha were in one small room, while Meghna and Akshay were in another.

Tired, hungry and with nowhere to go, Meghna sat on the bed, and then noticed Akshay purposefully looking around the small room and bathroom.

'What do you want, Akshay?' she whispered, as sounds of frantic running and screaming were heard outside. Akshay hushed her with a finger on his lips as he climbed the lone chair, pulled out the thick wooden curtain rod and then stood in front of their door. Meghna watched the back of her lanky fourteen-year-old holding the rod, intently assessing the sounds of danger just outside. He remained alert and watchful even after police whistles were heard and all became quiet. She realized that day that the roles had reversed. Her son Akshay, the little boy she had been looking after all these years, had now taken it upon himself to protect his mother from danger.

* * *

When the twins finished Class X and the results were awaited, Girish decided it was the right time for a long family holiday. Akshay and Neha were excited at the opportunity to go abroad and spend time with their cousins in the US. As a father, Girish also wanted them to see a bit of the world and felt the exposure would help them gain knowledge about opportunities for higher education and future career options. It was a memorable holiday with extended family travelling from New York to Los Angeles and of course, the thrill of experiencing a different country. The twins had a whale of a time with their cousins, the highlight being their visits to exciting theme parks with their thrilling rides.

* * *

On the flight back, Akshay rested his head on Meghna's shoulder and said, 'It was a great holiday, ma, and maybe we will travel again, but I would like to study and stay in India.'

Meghna understood that her son knew what he wanted and wouldn't be changing his mind.

After completing Class XII, Akshay, who was determined to join the forces, appeared for the NDA exam and cleared it in one go. Sons rarely follow advice, but usually do emulate the examples their fathers set for them. In Girish, he had not only seen an excellent father, but also an ace pilot and Akshay was determined to be a fighter pilot just like his father.

Akshay's first choice therefore was the air force in the NDA and he sailed through the Pilot Aptitude Test in the SSB. But he couldn't clear the stringent medical test for perfect eyesight, and his passion and dream of becoming a pilot like his father, crashed.

Girish, who was flying commercial planes at that time, suggested that Akshay join a civil aviation course instead of going to the NDA. But Akshay's passion for the armed forces and the uniform was much greater than his passion to be in the cockpit.

If not a pilot like his father, Akshay would follow in the footsteps of his grandfather and become a part of the great Indian Army. What if the colour of his uniform would now be olive instead of blue? He would still be serving his motherland.

Chapter 7

Are You Crazy?

It was the morning of 29 November 2016 when Maj. Kunal received a call from his buddy Lakhwinder Singh.

'Who is calling at five-thirty in the morning?' he murmured, looking at the clock mounted on the wall.

Just then, his wife, Uma's, phone also rang. It was Anju Raina, the wife of Lt Col Ravi Raina, who was the second-in-command (2IC) but performing the duty of officiating commanding officer, as Commanding Officer (CO) Col Prakash, was on leave.

'Why is Mrs Raina calling so early in the morning?' Uma was startled. Even before they picked up their respective phones, they knew that something wasn't right.

It had just been a day since they had returned from a month's leave to Kunal's hometown, Pandharpur. He wanted to celebrate Diwali with his family and insisted on taking a picture together. He had wanted the picture since he hadn't had the chance to have the entire family together for a while. He didn't miss the opportunity during that Diwali. Kunal's leave wasn't over yet. He was supposed to join a day later, but they had decided to return early so that they could get back to their routine after almost a month's break.

* * *

There are people who want to spend their lives with someone special, and then there are those who want to spend their lives with someone who becomes special. Kunal fell in the latter group.

A posting to Ladakh or its whereabouts is not unusual for a young officer in the Indian Army. Kunal loved the mountains and trekking there was a sort of meditation for him, though he couldn't manage to go on any treks due to his busy schedule. There was something mystical about the barren mountains of Ladakh. The colour of the craggy peaks set them apart. The landscape was made up of purple, yellow, orange and pink hues. Kunal's intense and passionate nature made him deeply appreciate the place and he wanted to share his emotions with someone. But after two terrible break-ups, he had stopped trusting women. When your experiences are based on repeated lies, you lose faith.

* * *

There is only one rule to taking leave in the army—when you get it, take it. When Kunal's leave was sanctioned by his CO, he headed to his hometown, Pandharpur—a pilgrimage town situated on the banks of the Chandrabhaga River. It is also called south Kashi in Maharashtra. The Vitthal temple there is quite famous, and various legends are associated with it, and it is visited by people from all over the world.

Kunal was very proud of his hometown's history and tradition. The faith with which the pilgrims visited his town was incredible and everything that Kunal did was infused with the same faith.

* * *

He had barely reached home when his family bombarded him with proposals of prospective brides. This is not unusual in an army officer's life. Just as good and evil go hand in hand, so did holidays and marriage, for a bachelor army officer. Kunal buckled under parental pressure and agreed to meet Uma and her family, who lived in the small town of Khapori. Kunal and his family travelled for almost four hours to see Uma. When Kunal saw Uma, he felt that the journey had been worth it. Uma didn't even take a minute to approve of Kunal as her life partner. She was pretty impressed by his personality but Kunal wanted to be absolutely candid about his life before Uma committed to him.

Uma was just twenty-two years old, studying business management when she met Kunal for the first time. It was December 2008, and the weather was quite pleasant in Khapori. Kunal chose to wear a checked shirt and denims, clothes he was most comfortable in. Uma was looking drop-dead gorgeous in a peach salwar kameez.

The family gave Kunal and Uma the time and space to speak and get to know each other.

Kunal wondered about the irony of arranged marriages. He had always wanted to marry someone he loved but he had given up on love. Yet, he wondered why couldn't he love the woman he married and lead a happy life? With this thought in mind, Kunal started the conversation with Uma.

'What do you do?' Kunal ended up asking a clichéd arranged-marriage question.

'I'm studying business management,' Uma answered meekly.

'What would you like to do after that?' Kunal was clear about the questions he was asking.

'Maybe a masters, diploma or . . .' Uma paused.

'Or what?'

'Or maybe get married,' Uma said shyly.

Kunal was quite amused. He wondered if women were still so excited about getting married the way Uma was. His past experiences had been somewhat different.

'What are your hobbies?' Kunal asked another clichéd question.

'I like to travel. What do *you* like doing?' Uma asked.

Kunal was a man of varied interests which Uma probably never pursued. So, he smiled and broke the ice. 'I like playing badminton and table tennis. I also like travelling and trekking in the mountains. Do you like mountains?'

'Yes! I do, but I haven't travelled much. My parents don't go out often and they don't allow me to travel unaccompanied,' Uma conversed innocently.

'Don't worry, you'll travel with me . . .' Kunal paused for a while and then added, 'A lot.'

Kunal knew the perils of being an army officer's wife but he didn't want to scare Uma at the outset. But travelling was not a part of the perilous life led by army people. There were bigger dangers in store for them.

The conversation changed track to friends, schooling and college education. And by the time they realized it, it was time for Kunal and his family to leave. Kunal bid goodbye to Uma and promised to meet her again.

When Uma was asked if she liked Kunal, she instantly said yes. Her answer was conveyed to Kunal's paternal aunt who had brought the proposal.

Uma and Kunal continued to speak over the phone to get to know each other better. Uma, in her heart and mind, had accepted Kunal as her husband, but Kunal was still waiting—waiting for Uma to accept him after he told her everything she needed to know before starting a life with him.

* * *

Kunal had met Uma in December 2008 when he got leave to visit his parents. But he was so eager to meet her again that he applied for leave the very next month. The rest of his family was equally excited to meet Uma.

Uma was studying in Pune and staying at her maternal aunt's place. It was decided the entire family would travel to Pune to meet Uma.

* * *

Kunal had spoken a lot to Uma over the phone but there were certain things he wanted to tell her in person. Kunal wore his favourite white shirt and denims to look his best. Clothes were the last thing Kunal needed to impress Uma as she was already head over heels in love with him.

Kunal and his family finally reached Pune and went to Uma's *maasi*'s place. The members of the family who had not met Uma had many questions for her: *Did she know how to cook? Did she like travelling? Did she like pets?* And so on.

Anybody familiar with Kunal knew that he was a big foodie who liked to try every new cuisine and dish. He loved travelling and pets as well. His family was keen to know Uma's interests and there seemed to be no end to their barrage of questions.

***

Kunal didn't seem to be getting the chance to speak to Uma alone. He was waiting for someone in the room to say, 'Uma, why don't you take Kunal to your room?' Just then, as if it was an answer to his prayers, Uma's maasi emerged as an angel and said, 'Uma, why don't you take Kunal to your room?' Kunal almost sprang up from his chair in excitement.

Uma took Kunal to her room and asked him to sit on the only chair in the room while she sat on the bed. She suddenly seemed even more beautiful to Kunal than she had been in the living room, dressed in a cream salwar kameez with a matching dupatta. Often, Kunal had imagined her in a similar attire, and for a moment he sat transfixed by Uma's beauty. He completely forgot why he had come to see her. He was startled out of his reverie when Uma reminded him, 'You wanted to say something important to me over the phone?'

'Oh! Yes. A lot of things, in fact.'

He folded his hands, looked at the floor and leaned forward. He then looked up at Uma and said, 'Don't be upset with whatever I tell you, but I want to be honest at the outset. I can't have a relationship based on lies and deceit.'

Though Uma was nonplussed, Kunal continued, 'I give a lot of importance to relationships and I want to have one with you.'

Hearing this, Uma relaxed.

'I've been in two relationships earlier—one in school and one in college, but they didn't materialize.'

Uma was glad and thought those women had been fools to let go of someone like Kunal.

'But I promise that you will never hear about them again after our marriage. All the same, it was important that you know this.'

Uma listened to Kunal patiently and was wondering why a handsome man like him had had only two relationships. He was the kind of guy any girl would like to be in a relationship with.

'I'm glad you told me the truth.' Uma was floored by his honest confession.

Kunal was relieved to hear that. He could now step up the game of knowing if Uma wanted to get married to him as madly as he wanted to get married to her. He wanted to know Uma's eagerness to be his life partner.

'Do you know anything about army life?'

Though Uma shook her head signalling a big no as no one in her family had ever been in the army, she showed her willingness to learn saying, 'I'm fascinated by whatever I've seen about the Indian army in movies—the uniforms and the locations.'

Kunal looked at her and said, 'The Indian army is much more than uniforms and locations, and the job of an army wife is sometimes more important than the job of an officer. I'm not trying to scare you, but you need to understand the hardships of being the wife of an Indian soldier. You will be subjected to multiple relocations every two to three years. You may sometimes be expected to live alone, you may be highly underemployed and may experience the stress of the unknown. And for that, you'll have to be adaptable and resilient. I'm committed to the greater cause of the security of my country, my men, and only then comes my commitment to you. Are you ready to be my wife?' Kunal ended with a smile.

'What do you mean by the stress of the unknown?' Uma asked innocently as she had understood everything else except that.

'I could come home wrapped in a tricolour,' Kunal said bluntly.

'Please don't say that!' Uma's eyes welled up instantly.

Kunal got up from the chair and gave Uma a warm hug. And it was enough for both of them to realize that they were ready to be man and wife.

* * *

After spending a few more days with his family, Kunal returned to work, happy and satisfied. But he remained very distracted as he longed to be with Uma. He wanted to get married to her at the earliest. While he was dreaming of building a home with Uma, his parents were matching their horoscopes. To Kunal's surprise, their horoscopes didn't match and his parents cancelled the marriage. Kunal was terribly upset as he didn't want anything in his

Maj. Kunal Gosavi with Uma and their daughter, Umang

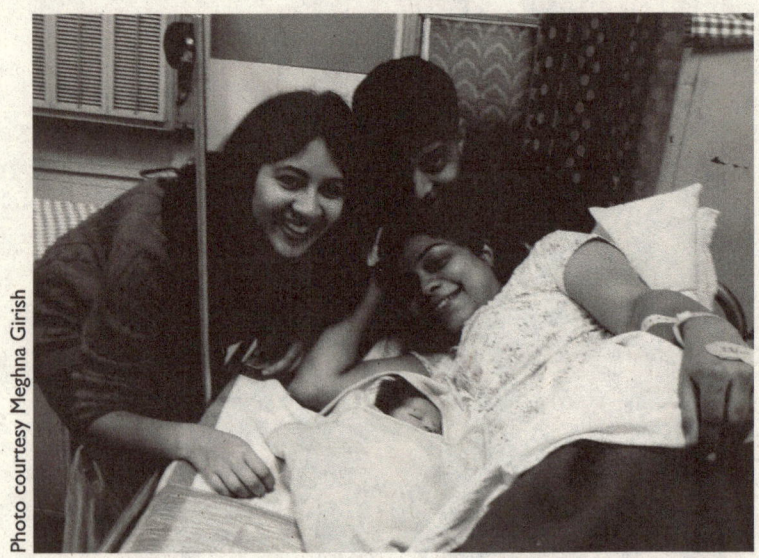

Maj. Akshay Girish with his sister Neha and wife Sangeeta after
the birth of his daughter Naina

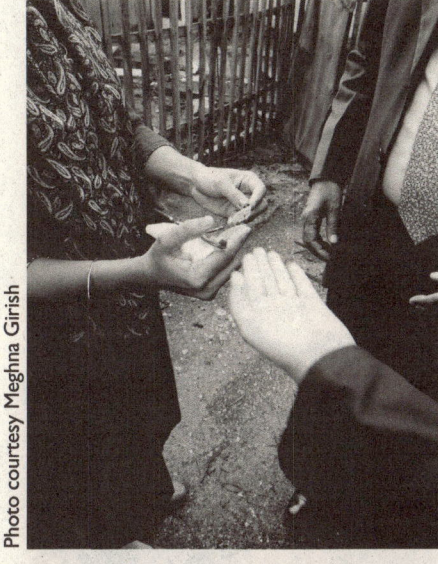

Photo courtesy Meghna Girish

Akshay's family finds his spectacles at the incident site where his body was found

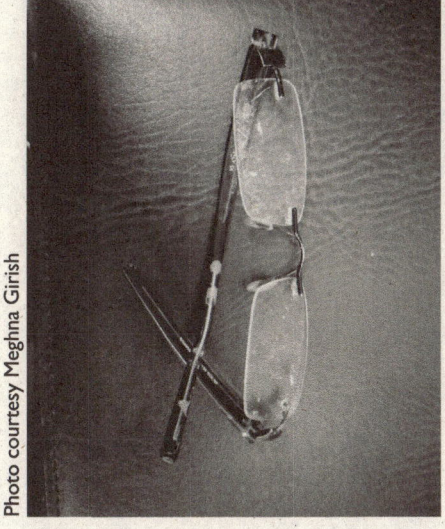

Photo courtesy Meghna Girish

Akshay's broken spectacles, recovered by his family from the site where he fought bravely

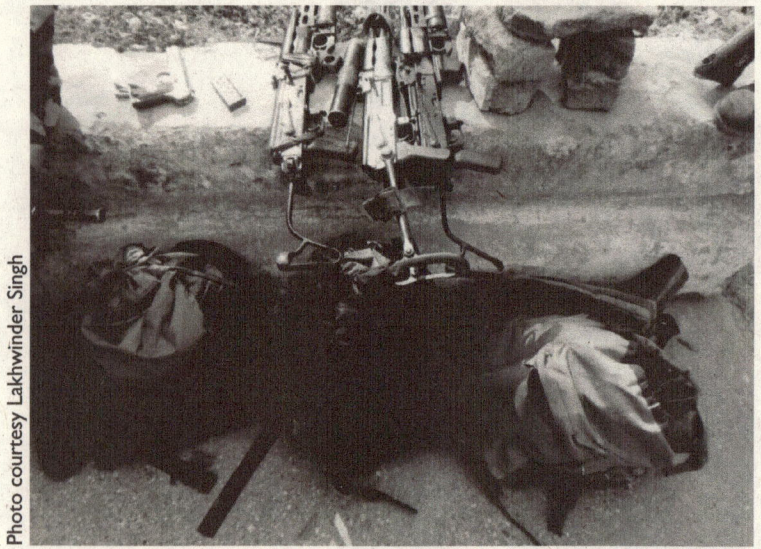

The weapons and bags that were carried by the fidayeens

The destruction of the building where Maj. Vinod and his family, Capt. Mukul, Lt Himanshu and Maj. Deepak lived

The items that were inside the bags of the fidayeens

Photo courtesy Lakhwinder Singh

Naik Lakhwinder Singh, who played a key role in the Nagrota siege. He also visited the attack site with the author to provide her a pictorial description of the events, as described by various sources.

Meenu and her daughter
Amayra after being
rescued by paratroopers

A recent picture of Naik Chittaranjan Debbarma's
parents, his wife Namita and children Inlet
and Kuplai

life as badly as he wanted Uma. He had let go of his love of sports, his participation in the Republic Day parade and one year of his professional life due to his family's insistence, but this time there was no way he was going to let go of Uma. In just a few days, he had become very fond of her and if he ever wanted anything passionately in life, it was Uma. He was ready to go to any extent to have her in his life.

Realizing that Uma would know that the horoscopes hadn't matched, he called her up.

'Don't worry, I'll handle it,' he told a dejected Uma.

'Your parents are saying that this marriage is not possible, how will *you* handle it?' she asked him sadly.

'As long as I'm there, you don't have to worry. If I marry, it'll only be to you or else I'll remain a bachelor. Trust me, my parents certainly wouldn't want that!'

They both smiled and the tension was diffused slightly.

'Do you really like me so much?' Uma wanted added assurance.

Kunal sighed and said, 'When I came to visit you for the second time, I'd given you a commitment. I am a man who lives by my actions and not words. I *will* most certainly marry you.'

'That doesn't answer my question.' Uma persisted.

'Why would I want to marry you so desperately if I didn't like you? Does that answer your question?' Uma was happy to hear him say that.

'Just in case my parents don't agree, will you be willing to run away with me?' Kunal continued earnestly.

'I can't do that. My family will be very hurt and I'm not willing to hurt my family for my happiness.'

Kunal got the message loud and clear. He knew the best way to approach this operation was only by convincing his parents. And he managed to do it. He had given up a lot of things for their happiness so he knew it was going to be a well-earned bargain.

***

When Kunal would be sent on temporary duties (TDs) by his commanding officer, he would make a request to send him to Pune, so that he could meet his lady love. Once on a last-minute plan, on TD, he called up Uma from Leh airport and asked her to come to Pune to meet him.

'What will I tell my parents?' Uma was scared.

'That's your problem. You make your own excuses, but I'm coming to see you.' Kunal kept talking to her from the time he received his boarding pass until he boarded the flight.

Uma didn't know what to say. She was already thinking about the reasons she would give her family so that they'd let her travel all the way to Pune to meet Kunal. She too was no less eager to meet him but lacked the courage and the experience. She had never travelled alone in her life.

'It's time for my flight. I'll have to hang up. I'll call you as soon as I reach Chandigarh.'

Kunal hung up before his flight took off for Chandigarh. At Chandigarh, he realized there was no flight to Pune until late evening, so he decided to take a flight to Mumbai.

He called up Uma who had already told her parents that she was going to meet Kunal's sister-in-law in Pune.

She boarded a bus to Pune. She was familiar with Pune as she had spent her college years there while doing BEd.

'I'm already on my way to Pune. I'm almost half way there!' Uma exclaimed in excitement.

'Now, take a bus to Mumbai and meet me there,' Kunal insisted.

'Are you crazy?'

'Yes, for you!'

These electrifying words were enough to make Uma blush.

Kunal boarded the flight to Mumbai and Uma got off at the bus stand in Pune. Kunal's desire to meet Uma had rubbed off on her too and she hopped on to the next bus to Mumbai.

She had never done the crazy things that Kunal was making her do. But these things were making her feel empowered and independent.

Before she knew it, she was at the Mumbai bus stand. She waited there for Kunal to arrive from the airport. The moment she saw Kunal's cab pull up just next to her, her face lit up. Her heart raced and with a welcoming smile, she hugged Kunal and whispered, 'You're crazy!'

'You're officially one step closer to being an army wife. You've learnt to travel alone!'

Those were Kunal's small ways of making Uma independent because he knew that he was not always going to be there for her. She would be expected to live alone when Kunal would be going on field postings.

***

Kunal would not miss a chance to meet Uma whenever he could squeeze in a TD. Eventually, in December 2009, they tied the knot and became man and wife. Uma still had a few months to complete her BEd but that didn't keep them from going on their honeymoon to Mussoorie. Making memories was important to Kunal.

Uma completed her BEd and got ready to join Kunal in Sagar where she was going to get a unique welcome she had no idea about. The officers and women of Kunal's regiment were all geared up to play a prank on Uma.

Kunal, like a thorough gentleman, went to pick up his wife from her hometown. When the couple arrived at the railway station in Sagar, a few officers dressed as jawans walked in and took Kunal away, leaving Uma alone. She managed to haul the luggage on her own. Then she spotted a couple of women dressed like villagers who were standing there to receive her at the platform. They helped her with the luggage.

She was then asked to get into a two-ton army vehicle—a Shaktimaan truck. The truck didn't have a stair assembly and it was quite a task for anyone to climb into it. But Uma was sprightly and effortlessly jumped up and got in, while it was a real struggle for the other ladies. The prank boomeranged on the pranksters. Once they all got into the vehicle, the driver drove them to the officers' mess.

* * *

As Uma entered the mess, she noticed a video camera mounted on the top of a door pelmet facing the sofa she was asked to sit on.

Anju Raina, Maj. Ravi Raina's wife, came up to Uma and whispered, 'Your husband is not an officer, but a jawan in the Indian army. He has lied to you.'

Uma looked at Anju contemptuously and was angry that her loving husband Kunal was being called a liar.

'He could be a jawan, but certainly not a liar,' Uma asserted and then continued in her husband's defence, 'and I've seen pictures of the CO putting stars on his shoulders. I think you're gravely mistaken.'

Seeing the prank falling flat in the face of Uma's resolve, the team of players had to quickly come up with something new. They signalled each other and stepped out of the mess. After about ten minutes of animated discussion outside, they came up with a new plan.

'Where is Kunal?' Uma asked, watching the women walk towards her.

'He is closeted with his first wife. We're sorry. But didn't he tell you that he's a married man?' Anju pretended to be serious.

Instead of losing her calm as the pranksters thought she would, Uma gave all of them a sympathetic look. She was sure that they had lost the plot and needed some kind of treatment.

She pointed at the camera and smiled, 'But what's that camera doing on the door?'

The women looked at each other in embarrassment. They had been caught out by the smart young girl. All the pranks they tried to play, failed to even make a dent in Uma's trust in her husband. And from thereon began a story—of true love, selfless sacrifice, mutual respect and care.

Chapter 8

I'll Never Let You Fall, My Love

Sangeeta was woken up by the sound of a loud blast on the dark morning of 29 November 2016. Their three-year-old daughter Naina was sleeping sandwiched between her parents. Maj. Akshay, who was up to get ready for PT, had gone to the bathroom after positioning a pillow in his place; he didn't want to let Naina feel her father's absence. Sangeeta, who was worried about her daughter's sleep getting disturbed, quickly placed two cushions over her ears. She then got up from the bed and went into the living room to find out what was happening outside.

The couple, along with their daughter, were planning to travel to Mumbai that day to be with their parents, Meghna and Wing Commander Girish, to attend a close friend's wedding. Their bags were packed and Akshay's leave had been sanctioned a few days ago.

* * *

While on leave from the NDA, Akshay loved to play basketball in the National Games Village (NGV) in

Bengaluru with his friends. Only playing basketball though, wasn't enough for the raging hormones in a young boy of eighteen. He was attracted to a girl, Rubina, who knew nothing about basketball or Akshay's feelings for her. He found her cute and every time he scored a basket, he looked at her to see if she was impressed. But her expressions did not reveal anything.

But with Sangeeta, another girl on the scene, things were just the opposite. She asked Akshay's friend Aman, 'Who's this boy?'

She was so smitten by his infectious smile that just couldn't take her eyes off him and confessed to Aman, 'He is incredibly cute.'

Sangeeta clearly guessed that he had to be a *fauji* as his *katora* haircut was a dead giveaway. No sane person at that age would have a haircut like that. But Akshay carried it with a lot of panache. Instead of feeling like the odd man out, he would make people around him feel bohemian.

Sangeeta, by calling Akshay cute, had in a way chosen Aman to be her messenger. After Akshay and his team defeated the opposing team, they all went out for a coffee. Every boy had a bike and asked a girl to be his pillion. Sangeeta was hoping with all her heart that Akshay would ask her to be his pillion. When you are attracted to someone, nature manifests in your favour. This is what happened with Sangeeta that day. Akshay's bike didn't start and so his pillion left with someone else. Sangeeta grabbed the opportunity, recognizing the potential to further friendship and intimacy. Being a gentleman, Akshay, though sad about not being able to take Rubina, took Sangeeta instead to the coffee shop and also dropped her back. He was tempted to take Rubina on his bike on the way back, but since he had taken on the responsibility of Sangeeta, he decided to take it all the way. He was never happy about leaving things midway. He either didn't start and when he did, he always took it to the finish.

* * *

That day, Sangeeta was formally introduced to Akshay. He seemed like a boy full of life and love, and ethical as well. He had a positive aura that attracted everyone to him like pigeons flying towards grain.

Their next meeting took place when the whole group decided to go watch the movie *Lakshya*. Akshay offered to take Sangeeta on his bike. Sangeeta sheepishly held the backrest of the bike to steady herself but Akshay insisted, 'Hold me or you'll fall off.'

Sangeeta reluctantly held Akshay and felt safe as they zipped to the mall where the movie was playing. There was not much chatting during the movie but the ambience, the company and the love story of Preity Zinta and Hrithik Roshan in the movie had Cupid flying around Sangeeta and Akshay. Akshay took the lead and held Sangeeta's hand. Sangeeta didn't mind it at all and was ready to give their love story a start.

It was only at the end of the movie that Akshay said, 'You'll see me fight for my country like this one day.'

Sangeeta knew where he was coming from. She had seen her father, and had spent her entire life in the midst of soldiers.

* * *

Though Akshay had had feelings for Rubina earlier, he never told Sangeeta about it. His relationship with Sangeeta was effortless, and they didn't have to try very hard to be with each other. Before they knew it, they were dating. Coffees, samosas, flowers and gifts followed.

* * *

Akshay's second-term break was coming to an end. And before he left for the NDA, he came to meet Sangeeta at the NGV, close to her parents' house. Sangeeta sneaked out of her house with the excuse that she was going out for a walk.

Sangeeta had mixed reactions as she approached Akshay. She was happy that he had come to see her, but clearly very unhappy about him leaving.

They hugged each other and Akshay wrote his academy's address on a piece of paper and handed it over to Sangeeta.

'What is this?' Sangeeta asked.

'My address. I hope you will write to me,' Akshay was a little pensive.

'You don't have a phone?' Sangeeta was surprised.

'Not until I finish second term. But letters are always more welcome than calls. Your words will help me sail through the tough times. And whenever I need them, I can turn to your letters.' Akshay took Sangeeta's hand in his and kissed it. He then got out his passport-size photo and gave it to Sangeeta asking, 'Can I have one of yours?'

'What?' Sangeeta exclaimed.

'A photograph?' Akshay said with his hand stretched out.

'I don't have one right now, but I promise I'll send you one,' Sangeeta assured him, bidding a final goodbye with the hope they would meet soon.

* * *

After a few weeks, Sangeeta and her parents went to Darjeeling for a holiday. When she was getting herself photographed striking different poses, her parents were left wondering as to why she was insisting on so many pictures being taken. After these were developed, she chose one and sent it to Akshay with a letter.

Getting letters from Sangeeta was like a cooling shower on a hot sunny day. The exchange of letters continued for a few months, but then stopped all of a sudden. When Akshay didn't call or send a message, Sangeeta became very anxious. But she had no way of contacting him. She felt guilty, wondering if she had done anything wrong to make Akshay ghost her.

* * *

Sangeeta cried her heart out until her tears dried. Finally, she made peace with the fact that Akshay was clearly not interested in speaking to her any longer, whatever the reason. With great difficulty she tried to move on, until one day on New Year's Eve, she saw Akshay at the Army Club where she had gone with her parents. Her heart skipped a beat while looking at him. Akshay spotted her too, and wanted to speak to her but didn't have the courage. He sent a message through his friend, Aman.

'Hi Sangeeta!' Aman approached her.

She replied coldly, 'Hi.'

'Akshay wants to speak to you but is scared you may take off your sandal and beat him with it.'

Sangeeta couldn't hide her amusement and laughed.

'Can he speak to you?' Aman asked.

'Of course, he can!' Sangeeta was euphoric as she was curious to know what had gone wrong and why he had stopped speaking to her. If nothing else, she wanted closure.

That evening Akshay called up Sangeeta, 'I'm leaving for the academy soon. Can we meet tonight for coffee?' Akshay asked.

'I can't, Akshay. I've to go back with my parents. Maybe next time when you're on leave, we can talk.'

Sangeeta wasn't avoiding Akshay. She had protective parents who wouldn't allow their daughter out late at night, especially with a boy.

'Will you write to me?' Akshay asked.

Sangeeta didn't reply as all the memories of the hard times she faced came back.

'We can talk once you come home on your next leave.'

Sangeeta wasn't sure what kept her from speaking to Akshay that night but it worked as it made Akshay very restless. It was karma at its best. Akshay was struggling to talk to Sangeeta. He wasn't a boy anyone could be angry with for long as he was charming, loving and honest, apart from having a killer smile.

* * *

The next time Akshay was on leave, the first thing he did was meet Sangeeta and speak to her. With an apology in his eyes and a smile on his face, he reached Sangeeta's house and spoke his heart out, 'You deserve to know the reason for my strange behaviour. I'm very sorry to have kept you in the dark. I was confused. I was dealing with feelings I never had before. I couldn't be frank with you as I wasn't sure if I was ready for a commitment . . .'

Sangeeta cut him short.

'Do you like Rubina?'

'No, no, no. It's all in the past now. I like only you. I feel at peace with you. I waited as I had to be sure before I could make a commitment to you.'

'Are you sure now?' Sangeeta asked firmly.

'That's why I've come to you,' Akshay replied earnestly.

And after that honest confession, there never were any major roadblocks.

* * *

Sangeeta moved to Jaipur for her MBA, while Akshay graduated from the Indian Military Academy after NDA, and joined his unit in Nagaland. His entry into 51 Engineer Regiment started with the traditional welcome of '51 Punch' that knocked teetotaller Akshay out and sent him into a deep drunken slumber! From the next morning, he had seniors guiding him on operating in the insurgency-affected areas of Nagaland and Manipur. The invaluable experience taught him early on the inherent risks and dangers of the profession, yet bolstered his courage and reinforced his commitment to the country.

* * *

When his unit moved to Zirakpur, a peace posting, he took on his company's task of fencing along the Line of Control beyond Tangdhar in Kupwara, J&K. Attached to an infantry unit, Akshay motivated his men and worked with them to complete the fencing overnight under dim torchlight. The next day, he requested to be included in the infantry patrol. The patrol had a long wait all night in pin-drop silence. In the early hours, when the terrorists came, expecting a gap in the fence, they were caught by surprise and eliminated by a fusillade of expertly aimed gunfire. Young Akshay made good use of the AK-47 in his first real experience of battling the enemy. The infiltration bid was successfully foiled. Akshay volunteering for patrolling and his bravery that night were appreciated by the Infantry CO and the brigade commander.

* * *

After a few months, he managed to take leave to be with Sangeeta. It had been five years since they had known each other and almost four since they had been dating. It was time for Akshay to take the relationship to the next level. For that, he planned a trip with Sangeeta to Shimla without their parents getting wind of it. He planned to propose to Sangeeta on that trip. His way of doing things was always extravagant. If anyone had taken Karan Johar's movie *Kal Ho Na Ho* to heart, it was Akshay. He wanted to do everything that day and go big.

He got a ring for Sangeeta and planned a dinner at a five-star hotel. But as soon as they reached the hotel in Shimla, they were informed that there was a curfew in the city. Akshay saw all his plans crumble. But he wasn't the sort to give up. He stopped his car at a beautiful spot on a hilly road and asked Sangeeta to step out. Sangeeta thought that he wanted to admire the beautiful sunset. After getting out of the car, he stood facing Sangeeta. He went down on one knee and took out a pen drive that was attached to a ring from his pocket and said, 'Will you marry me?'

Sangeeta was overjoyed. She didn't care about the location, the pen drive ring or the dinner fiasco; she was completely bowled over. She had received a proposal from the man with whom she longed to spend the rest of her life. She was on cloud nine and yelled, 'Yes, my love!'

The next big move was to disclose their relationship to their parents.

'Will your parents have any problem with me asking for your hand?' Akshay asked with a frown.

'My dad is a South Indian, but wouldn't mind marrying me off to a sardar as long as he is in the army. He believes that if the government can trust a man with the country, he can definitely trust him with his daughter. Believe me, they will have no problem at all.'

Sangeeta was sure of her family.

'Then I need to bell the cat soon.' Akshay had already started working on a plan to be with the love of his life at the earliest. The only thing in the way of his marriage was his twin sister Neha whom he loved dearly. There was no way he was getting married before she did, but he knew Neha didn't have anyone special in a radius of a hundred feet. At twenty-four, she had started working after her masters in the US and didn't even want to get married. So, when she came to know that her brother wanted to get married, she convinced everybody to let Akshay get married before she did. Although Akshay was with his unit and Sangeeta in Hyderabad beginning her first job, a meeting was soon set up by Akshay and Sangeeta over phone calls, for their respective parents to meet each other at the Army Club in Bengaluru.

* * *

When the two officers met each other, they reminisced about defence services, their coursemates, common friends and so on, over a couple of drinks. In other words, everything but their children. Knowing this could happen when two officers met, Akshay had told his mother Meghna to talk about his courtship with Sangeeta.

So Meghna initiated the dialogue, 'I think we are meeting for our children. They have decided to be with each other and Girish and I have no objections. Hope you are also willing!'

'Of course we are! I mean, Akshay is a fine boy. Let's formalize the proposal as soon as possible,' Sangeeta's father gave his consent with a guffaw.

Sangeeta and Akshay got the go-ahead and the proposal got a formal stamp of approval. They were engaged and the courtship lasted for another year before they finally got married. In the meantime, Akshay moved to Pune for his BTech at the College of Military Engineering (CME).

When Sangeeta joined Akshay in Pune after their wedding, she received a royal welcome by Akshay's coursemates. He knew that he was going to be sacrificed at the altar of marriage, but didn't know it was going to happen in such a manner.

Sangeeta and Akshay were invited to the mess for dinner. At the gate, they were asked to get out of their car. They saw an empty vegetable cart decorated with balloons. Sangeeta was made to sit in the cart and Akshay was asked to push it until the entrance of the mess. His coursemates walked alongside the cart blowing trumpets. But it didn't end there—Akshay was made to glug single malt whisky out of a bottle—neat.

Akshay was not very fond of drinking, and he would nurse one glass of single malt all through a party. He liked to savour his drink and knew his limits. But that day, there was clearly none. He had to chug down almost an entire bottle before the party had even started.

'Now, you have to pick her up and take her inside. Her feet shouldn't touch the ground until she is seated in a chair,' his coursemates instructed.

Akshay lifted her up and started walking gingerly towards the mess.

'I'll fall!' Sangeeta kept whispering in his ear while masking her nervousness with a charming smile.

'I'll never let you fall, my love.' Akshay held her tight and only let her go when he put her down on a chair.

Everyone cheered for the newlyweds. That night was full of love, life and new beginnings for the starry-eyed couple.

* * *

Though Akshay had got the house ready for Sangeeta, she spent the next few months decorating it to her taste. She also took up a job in Pune. A month after their wedding, a new member was welcomed to the family—Bingo, a cocker spaniel. They had visited a kennel just to see puppies, but they returned not only with a pup, but also a bunch of accessories needed to raise that little addition to the family. Now, Bingo governed their life. They avoided late-night parties, woke up on time for his walk and loved him unconditionally. Bingo reciprocated with double that love.

* * *

It was only after they had mastered the art of being good parents to Bingo that they decided to move ahead and have a baby. Bringing up Bingo gave them that confidence. Akshay loved babies and now they felt they were ready to take on the responsibility.

Taking it one step at a time, the couple was excited nonetheless to learn they would be parents soon. Sangeeta was pregnant after almost two years of marriage. The first four months were a little tough for Sangeeta as she had developed hypertension. She left for Bengaluru to be with her mother so that she could be looked after. The doctor had asked her to rest, so she quit her job before she could be tied down by travel restrictions. Akshay couldn't visit her often due to his exams, but he made it a point to come for Sangeeta's *sreemantham* (baby shower). In fact, his parents had planned the baby shower in the seventh month because that was the only time Akshay could get leave.

'I'm sure it's a girl,' Akshay would often tell Sangeeta and his mother Meghna. He so desperately wanted a little girl, that the thought of Sangeeta delivering a boy never crossed his mind.

'What if it's a boy?' Sangeeta asked him, worried.

'It's not possible. I'm sure it's a girl,' Akshay said as if he was sure of being blessed and of his wish coming true.

* * *

The next two months went by in a jiffy and Akshay came to Bengaluru before the due date. Due to Sangeeta's hypertension, she had to be hospitalized two weeks before the due date. Unlike other civil hospitals, none of the family members were allowed to stay with the mother-to-be in the hospital. At night, the doctors went off duty, leaving the patients in the ward under the care of interns. Sangeeta remained anxious with a prenatal non-stress test machine hooked up to her stomach.

An intern stopped by and started telling her stories about his posting in Dimapur.

'You know, there is a snake market in Dimapur.'

Sangeeta was getting more anxious, and was least interested in the stories that he was telling her. The intern wanted to keep her awake so he could regularly monitor the baby's heartbeat. When he felt there was none, he asked her to get up and start walking. She walked for a while and when she lay down again, he took out his basic mobile phone, put it on Sangeeta's belly and made it vibrate. The baby's heartbeat resumed and the intern let out a sigh of relief.

* * *

In the morning, the doctor came on her rounds and examined Sangeeta. She then took an amniotic hook and broke Sangeeta's water bag artificially. Meanwhile, a team of interns had gathered around Sangeeta's legs, trying to learn about delivering a baby. Sangeeta was amused at the inquisitive interns, rather than being annoyed or embarrassed at having them hustling around her legs.

Naina was born after two hours of labour. As the nurse placed the baby on Sangeeta's stomach, she instantly forgot the pain she had been through. The happiness of holding that tiny human being made her forget the months of anxiety, sleepless nights and the labour she had gone through.

'Is it a boy or a girl?' Sangeeta asked the nurse breathlessly. When she said that it was a girl, Sangeeta told the nurse to call Akshay immediately.

'He always wanted a girl,' Sangeeta said.

* * *

Her family held the tiny bundle of joy in their arms one by one and the moment she opened her eyes, everyone called out in unison, 'Naina!' The name was in sync with the baby's beautiful, big eyes. A family fiesta followed.

The next day Akshay left for Pune to appear for his exams, while Sangeeta returned to her mother's house for the next forty days. After that, Sangeeta went to stay with her in-laws for some time before she returned to Pune. She was missing Akshay and wanted him to be with his little daughter for whom he had prayed day and night.

Naina received a grand welcome in Pune by Akshay's coursemates and Sangeeta's friends. From then on, life for the couple was mostly filled with sleepless nights, changing nappies and timing feeds. But along with that came even more love and a sense of completeness.

* * *

Akshay's next posting was back to his unit stationed at Kanchrapara near Kolkata. He was part of one of the oldest and most prestigious engineering units of the Indian Army. Sangeeta joined him later with baby Naina. She was happy that she'd finally be introduced to the unit this time. Akshay also had to start preparing for the Army Staff College in the coming year. It is one of the most difficult courses to get through and undoubtedly the most sought-after in the Indian Army. Akshay believed that he had to be in the system, and at the top, if he had to do good by his men. That motivated him to take his studies very seriously and he did well in all his courses.

* * *

Although a peace station, engineer regiments get specific tasks and Akshay and his company moved to high altitudes above 17,000 feet to build bunkers along the Line of Actual Control (LAC) with China. It was a challenging task and Akshay spent almost six months with his troops on snowy mountains, motivating them and ensuring their safety and welfare while working at treacherous heights. High-altitude sickness is a killer and heli-evacuation is not always possible when the weather worsens. When the task was safely completed well before time, he insisted on cooking dinner for all 120 of his men to appreciate their efforts. That chicken biryani with kaju masala cooked by Akshay is fondly remembered to this day by his men.

* * *

In October 2015, at Neha's wedding to Pradish, the usually smiling Akshay was emotional and everyone teased him about it. His eyes were bright with unshed tears to see his beloved sister as a beautiful bride. He penned a note to his brother-in-law telling him what a wonderful sister Neha had been and how lucky he was to have her as his wife. Soon after the wedding, in December 2015, Akshay's unit was going to celebrate its golden jubilee. Being the adjutant, Akshay was bestowed with the responsibility of making the event a success. Akshay was known to do things differently and he made a remarkable addition to the celebrations. That year, he laid the foundation of the wreath-laying ceremony for all those killed in action from his unit. He even dug out the details of those who had died in the 1965 and 1971 wars and honoured them on that special day. From that day onward, it would become a tradition on every Raising Day. Little did he know that his name was soon going to be etched with the others on the same epitaph.

* * *

To write that destiny, Akshay was posted to Nagrota in September 2016. Akshay decided to drive from Kanchrapara to Nagrota, rather than fly, as it was difficult for Bingo to travel by air. He planned a journey that would take six days from Kanchrapara to Nagrota.

'I've never seen the Taj Mahal,' Sangeeta said when she was told that they'd be crossing Agra to reach Nagrota.

'What? You've never seen the Taj Mahal?' Akshay was shocked to hear that as he had been to the Taj Mahal many times.

'Will we have the time to see it?' Sangeeta asked hopefully.

'We are only stopping for a few hours there, not even the entire day. Let me see what we can do to show you one of the wonders of the world.'

Akshay wanted Sangeeta to see the Taj Mahal but he hadn't figured out how to go about it.

When they reached Agra, Akshay took Sangeeta to the Taj Hotel's coffee shop from where they could get a clear view of the entire marble wonder.

They sat on the balcony, sipping coffee. Sangeeta was mesmerized by the beauty of the Taj, but even more by the way her husband had managed to fulfil her wish.

* * *

Akshay's effort to show Sangeeta the Taj Mahal was symbolic of the love he had for her. For Sangeeta, seeing the grand monument was not as important as the effort Akshay had made for her, and her love for him grew stronger than ever before.

Their next evening was spent at Akshay's coursemate's home in Amritsar and Meghna had told him not to miss paying respects at Harmandir Sahib.

'I don't know if we will have time, ma,' Akshay had said, but later called his mother from the Golden Temple to tell her how beautiful it was and how much at peace he felt. He thanked her for insisting they visit the famed place of worship. It was Akshay's last temple visit. Perhaps destiny drove him to get god's blessings before doing what was to come next.

Chapter 9

It's Just a Decanter

It was in March 2016 that the 166 Medium Regiment had all its officers and families come together in Nagrota. Prior to that, the unit was stationed in Sagar, a small city in Madhya Pradesh. Though there wasn't much to do in the city, the unit's activities kept the ladies busy and the officers had their regular duties to attend to. It was the early months of 2016 when they were informed that their regiment would soon be moving to Nagrota.

* * *

Lieutenant Mukul, a young Punjabi boy, joined the 166 Medium Regiment as a lieutenant in Sagar. He was a newbie and quite eager to prove his mettle. A nationalist, high on patriotism, he couldn't think of a profession better than being a soldier in the Indian Army.

* * *

Maj. Kunal was sent to his parent unit in Sagar after spending two years in the Assam Rifles. He had been a part of many successful operations in the Assam Rifles and had thoroughly enjoyed his role there. Kunal was very restless in Sagar—a peace posting with a desk job was just not for him. He wanted action. The sole purpose of joining the army was to show his valour in the battlefield. His restlessness spurred him to think of joining the National Security Guard (NSG). But his commanding officer advised him to have a normal and sane life for some time with his family. However, Maj. Kunal was cast in an altogether different mould and was known to turn batty if 'normal' lasted too long.

* * *

Maj. Vinod had joined the unit later; in July 2016. He had had his share of the Assam Rifles. Though he had faced less action than Kunal there, he was now a man with varied experiences. One may be a natural in the field of operations, having the passion and the skills for it, but nothing can beat the experience gained though serving in diverse roles and postings. Maj. Vinod was looking forward to this posting as he was hoping to get better accommodation for his family. Bhanupriya had stayed too long in makeshift accommodations all through Vinod's Assam Rifles tenure. Vinod felt that his family deserved better even if it was for a short while. Shreyasi, his little daughter, had just turned one and he wanted Bhanupriya and their baby to be comfortable. Just a reasonably decent house was their only requirement.

***

Capt. Deepak had always wanted to be a doctor. But he had also nurtured a wish to be in the army owing to his schooling in Army School, Mathura Cantonment. He had joined the school as a civilian but had always been fascinated by army life because that was all he saw, all the time around him. At the same time, as a child, he had seen his father treat patients. In a normal environment, an individual is greatly influenced and inspired by his surroundings and Deepak was no different. He completed his MBBS from Bishkek, the capital of Kyrgyzstan. And as soon as he returned to India, he started preparing for the SSB exam to get into the army. He passed with flying colours and was soon sent to Lucknow for his induction training. He was posted to Mathura's Strike Corps and served there for two years before he was given the news that he was to join the 166 Medium Regiment as the regimental medical officer (RMO).

***

After the announcement was made in the unit, while still at Sagar, everyone was quite excited to be going to Nagrota, a peaceful place close to the hills. An added reason for excitement was the possibility of being assigned specific operational tasks that usually came up close to the border in J&K.

Both Kunal and Mukul were Enfield enthusiasts, and just before leaving for Nagrota, had purchased two Royal Enfield Classic 350s. They had also got special registration numbers for their bikes: 5166 and 6166, with '166' symbolic of their unit number.

It was decided that Maj. Kunal and Lt Mukul would form the advance party.

'Cover the chromium parts with a foaming cushion. It'll prevent scratches,' was Kunal's advice to Mukul before they started packing. Maj. Kunal was responsible for taking over the assets, which are the stores, etc., from the relieving unit and understanding the role of their unit. Though in a desk job, he took his work very seriously and made all the arrangements for the rest of his unit to join him soon.

* * *

After a few weeks, Maj. Kunal had Lt Col Ravi Raina, who was joining his parent unit from Faridkot, by his side. Whereas Kunal saw his dreams of being in the midst of field action receding in the background, Ravi was happy to be posted to Nagrota. He saw this as an opportunity to be with his family. Anju, his wife, had taken up a job at the Government Women's College Parade, Jammu, and was balancing her professional life with that of an army officer's wife pretty well. Lt Col Ravi had stayed in the field far too long and like any other soldier, he loved being present with his wife and growing boys.

* * *

Maj. Nandi, the senior-most bachelor of the unit, was living with his mother in Sagar. On his birthday, she would always string up balloons outside their house to Nandi's discomfiture, and he would grumble, 'I'm not a baby any more, ma. This is quite embarrassing.'

As soon as those balloons were put up, the ladies of the unit would go over to his place to wish him. They would be warmly welcomed by Nandi's mother who loved to chat and laugh with them. She kept her youthful feelings alive in the company of the young and vibrant women. But as fate would have it, Nandi's mother, whose health had always been an issue, fell sick and her condition deteriorated further. She had to be admitted to a command hospital for further treatment. Nandi decided to take her to the command hospital in Kolkata as she was suffering from interstitial lung disease (ILD), a life-threatening irreversible lung disease. Her days were numbered, but before anything happened to her, she wanted to see her son 'settled'. Like any other Indian mother, her definition of 'settling down' was to see him getting married. Nandi was the senior-most among the bachelors in the unit—not only in terms of seniority but also in terms of age. Though he was already thirty-five, he wanted more time before he could find someone of the same wavelength to be his true companion. In fact, Nandi had met a woman, Nisha, and was seriously contemplating marriage with her, but he still needed some time to be absolutely sure. But Nandi's mother didn't have that kind of time. When he showed Nisha's photographs to his mother, she was quite relieved to know that her son was at last giving marriage a serious thought.

Nandi lost his mother on 30 April 2016, which delayed joining his parent unit. He could come to Nagrota only in June after he completed his mother's last rites. Though Nandi missed his mother badly and it was a time of emotional turmoil for him, he regained his composure once he was back in the unit.

* * *

Lt Himanshu was the baby of the unit, its youngest officer. Nagrota was his first posting after the 'royal treatment' of three years in the NDA and a year in the IMA. Of course, royal treatment in an academy is different from what you'd get at a five-star hotel. It means miles of running, rolling on concrete, hundreds of push-ups and pull-ups, bareback horse-riding and long stretches of staying away from the family. Being a newbie, Himanshu was embracing a different culture and learning the ways of working in a unit. Training is never enough. You can do a lot if you go through it properly, but most of the knowledge is rooted in experience.

* * *

Himanshu and Deepak were allotted a flat in a block that housed four small flats. It was a nondescript construction, rectangular in shape, right opposite the officers' mess. The two flats on the ground floor opened up to a lawn each, and were separated by a staircase that led to the flats on the first floor and eventually to the terrace. Above the terrace there were water tanks and a security post where a light machine gun (LMG) was positioned with a guard. The verandas of the flats on top were screened from direct sight with walls, perforated with holes, ensuring ventilation and adequate privacy.

* * *

Nagrota was a modified field station. Since it was never a high security risk, the civil administration had let their guard down. Thick vegetation had come up outside the cantonment in and around that area and the nomadic *bakharwals* (a tribe of shepherds) were often seen roaming in and around the place with their sheep. The villagers would also often come to the area to collect wood for fuel for their kitchens.

* * *

The sentry gate to the 166 Medium Regiment unit was just off the national highway. Walking down the gate that was manned by 24/7 security, the complex had one block of quarters that housed four apartments. Deepak and Himanshu occupied the flat on the left that was on the ground floor. The one on the right was occupied by Mukul. The flat on the first floor directly above Deepak and Himanshu's flat was Vinod's, while the one on the right-hand side of the first floor was vacant. Behind this block were two guard rooms and a small room housing a generator.

* * *

There was another block that had a lawn in front. It housed two flats with a terrace. Maj. Shalini was on the first floor while Maj. Nandi occupied the one on the ground floor. It was surrounded by thick vegetation and trees. Across the road from the first block of flats, was a lawn with white rocks. It was next to the officers' mess, and separated from the road by a wide drain. Next to the mess was a temporary guest house built with tin walls and a tin roof. A wall, that was rather low, ran behind the two structures. And between the two, there was a big tree that grew just outside the wall. A hillock stood behind the wall, and at its top, one could stand and get a view of the entire station.

Maj. Ajay, along with his wife Meenu and eight-month-old daughter Amayra, stayed in that guest room.

* * *

Lt Col Ravi and Maj. Kunal and their commanding officer, Col Salvekar, were allotted accommodations some 10 km away from the officers' mess. They had permanent accommodations due to their seniority and the availability of houses, while the others had to adjust in the temporary quarters, right opposite the mess.

* * *

If 166 Medium Regiment was the engine, Salvekar was its driver. And he drove that engine pretty well. He was a dedicated officer who had amazing experience. He knew his men better than the men knew themselves, and that probably was his biggest strength. He was always

well-informed about what was going on in his unit. For
instance, he knew that Nandi needed help with his mother
and Himanshu was a new officer and needed proper
orientation and guidance; just as he knew that Kunal was
excellent in field operations and very stable. A mother loves
all her children equally, but she secretly has a favourite
one. Col Salvekar was that mother and Maj. Kunal that
favourite child. It was just that the other children didn't
know about it.

* * *

It was 10 September 2016, and Nandi's thirty-sixth
birthday. When he returned from office in the afternoon,
he was greeted by the sight of colourful balloons hung
outside his house. As he opened his front door, he saw the
rooms had been decorated with balloons and streamers. He
was overwhelmed.

To make sure that his mother's way of celebrating his
birthday was continued, all the ladies of the unit had planned
a surprise for him. He was grateful for the affection, though
he missed his mother immensely that day.

* * *

The same evening, all the officers and ladies met for a
get-together in the mess. It was not specially for Nandi's
birthday but he did get all the attention that day—wishes,
flowers and gifts. While the ladies sat around a round table,
the men gathered around the bar. Some had their poison
while others were just high on new experiences.

Mukul showed a picture to Kunal on his phone and both started chuckling.

'What is it?' Deepak asked.

He took the phone away from Mukul only to see a picture of himself and Himanshu, wearing only boxers. They were lying sprawled on cots in a camp in the desert where the unit was training, with sunburnt cheeks.

'When did you take this?' Mukul winked at him.

'Look at your tummy, doc. You really need to come for BPET,' Mukul said, pointing to Deepak's belly in the picture.

BPET is the Battle Physical Efficiency Test to check the physical ability of a candidate to take up military tasks. It includes a series of activities like a 5-kilometre run and a 60-metre sprint. In addition to climbing a vertical rope, it includes traversing a horizontal one. It also includes crossing a deep ditch. There are timings and standards for each test, and the candidates classify as 'Excellent', 'Good', 'Satisfactory' and 'Fail'.

Himanshu was unrelenting. He'd pull Deepak out of bed to be a part of the exercise. It usually happened thrice a month or more, depending on the recommendation of the commanding officer, and Col Salvekar would have it more often than not.

* * *

Just then Naik Lakhwinder, a sepoy who was looking after the bar, fumbled and broke a crystal decanter full of wine. The decanter was not only expensive but also had the regiment insignia carved on it. Sensing the gravity of incident, Maj. Kunal immediately went up and took the scared Lakhwinder to one side of the room, away from the other officers, especially the CO.

'I'm sorry sir! I didn't do it deliberately,' Lakhwinder apologized.

'Come on! It's just a decanter, not the prestige of our unit.' Kunal wrapped his arm around Lakhwinder and said, 'Put it on my mess bill.' Maj. Kunal had his man covered.

***

The women sat around chatting and catching up.

'Have you got her admitted into a school?' Anju asked Uma about her three-year-old daughter Umang.

'Yes, in the pre-primary school,' Uma told Anju.

'Which class are you in, Umang?' Anju asked Umang, caressing her head and cupping her face.

She looked at her mother and babbled, 'LKG, auntie. My school is called White Knight.' She was very excited about her new school.

'We've also enrolled her for dance classes. Kunal takes her there every evening,' Uma added excitedly.

Shreyasi, Vinod and Bhanupriya's daughter, was holding on to the table and trying to walk. Umang held her hand and helped her.

'She has started walking, Bhanupriya,' Anju was excited to see little Shreyasi walking.

***

After a round of chatting, drinks and sumptuous dinner, they bid goodbye to each other. Since Col Salvekar, Lt Col Ravi, Maj. Kunal and their families stayed away from the mess, they got ready to leave before the rest.

After the CO, Ravi and Kunal left, Mukul shouted, 'See you at the BPET tomorrow, doc!'

Capt. Deepak smiled as they all started walking home.

Chapter 10

The Kashmir Conundrum

On the morning of 29 November 2016, Naik Chittaranjan Debbarma was ordered to join Maj. Akshay's Quick Reaction Team (QRT). He prepared his rifle and got into the Casspir vehicle along with the other men. He was part of Akshay's unit. A resident of west Tripura, he was a painter in the Indian Army. He had applied for a loan to build his house in his village but it hadn't come through, so his leave was delayed by a few days. It was not a coincidence. He was destined to be by the side of his fellow soldiers when the country needed him the most.

***

For over seventy years, Kashmir has been the bone of contention between India and Pakistan. This proxy war has only led to the growth of disillusioned youth like Burhan Wani, encouraged by mercenaries who have no other interest but to keep the unrest in India alive. Burhan Wani was a terrorist and the Indian Army killed him on

8 July 2016, leading to unrest in the Valley once again. Wani's killing led to large-scale protests across the Valley, resulting in the death of almost 100 people, becoming one of the worst periods of unrest in the region since 2010.

In the same year, on 18 September, four terrorists attacked the Indian Army Brigade Headquarters in Uri, near the LoC. They hurled seventeen grenades in about three minutes, setting the tents in the rear administrative base camp on fire. Those seventeen grenades led to the death of nineteen army personnel and injured thirty others.

***

Maj. Akshay Girish was in Amritsar, en route to Nagrota, when the incident took place. He had halted at his coursemate's house for a break and both were intently watching the reports broadcast all over the news channels. When someone changed the channel, Akshay, an otherwise calm man, was incensed.

'Our soldiers are dying there at the hands of these Pakistanis, and you're changing the channel? How can you do that?'

Sangeeta had never seen Akshay in such an agitated state of mind. He was always very gentle and diplomatic.

'If I ever get a chance, I want to stuff them with bullets. The Indian Army has lost so many brave men.'

That kind of loss, unlike any other deprivation, is very personal to a soldier. And Akshay was no different.

***

Kunal, on the day of the Uri attack, came home late, carrying a bulletproof jacket. After placing it on the dining table, he went to the kitchen where Uma was making his favourite dishes—sabudana khichdi with thalipeeth, Maharashtrian delicacies. It had always been therapeutic for Kunal to watch his wife cook and he would often stand at the kitchen door and talk to her while she cooked his favourite dishes.

'How was your day?' Uma read the anguish writ large on her husband's face.

'I'm so pained by what happened in Uri today,' Kunal.

'Yes! I saw that in the news today. It was terrible!' Uma joined her husband as he mourned for the fallen men, and then broke the silence.

'Shall I serve dinner? I have made your favourite dishes—sabudana khichdi and thalipeeth.'

Uma walked towards the dining table with a bowl of hot khichdi in her hands. And as she was about to put it down on the table, she froze as she saw the jacket on the table.

'What's this doing here?'

Kunal looked at her and said, 'I want to be ready in case any orders come for us to go forward. Things are really boiling after this attack. I want to be the first to take that opportunity.'

A wish could be a blessing and sometimes a curse in disguise. Akshay, like Kunal, was impatiently looking for a chance to teach the perpetrators a lesson. But neither was aware that they were going to get that chance so soon.

* * *

Two days after the Uri attack, Akshay reached Nagrota with his family—Sangeeta, Naina and their dog Bingo. They were to stay in a guest room. In the afternoon after lunch, Akshay left for the pre-induction training to orient himself with the operational area. Though Akshay had been in the field in Sikkim, the tactical skills varied for each operational environment, and he along with the others, spent the next two weeks training from dawn to dusk at a battle school in the mountains of Kashmir. Sangeeta, meanwhile, was happy to see the familiar faces of Akshay's regiment and began settling down in her new environment.

* * *

The loss of lives of soldiers is taken very personally by a nation like India and more so by fellow soldiers.

'The bastards got into the Uri cantonment,' Chittaranjan said while having lunch in the *langar* with the other jawans of his unit.

'There must be a mole inside,' said another jawan.

'Not really! We have boundary walls extending up to tens of kilometres. If someone has to enter the cantonment, he can enter from anywhere. If someone has to drop a bomb or hurl a grenade, he doesn't even need to enter,' Chittaranjan said.

'Then why don't we have attacks taking place every day if it is so easy?' asked a new recruit.

'Because Pakistan knows that if they do, we will not only kill them but dig up their ancestors from their graves and kill them again. Just wait and see what the Indian Army does to them now after Uri. We will not take this lying down. We are not the same old defensive army now, buddy. We will respond in their language.'

'How?' asked the new recruit.

'We have a population of over 140 crore people. If only the men of the Indian Army that comprises more than 15 lakh soldiers stand at the border, open their flies and pee, Pakistan will become an extension of the Persian Gulf. We are talking of a nation that has been ranked as having the fourth-strongest army in the world, one that can defeat the strongest army any day with hand-to-hand combat.'

The other jawans laughed with a sense of pride at Chittaranjan's words.

* * *

After eleven days of foolproof intelligence inputs, preparation and teamwork, India conducted surgical strikes on 29 September 2016 on militant launching pads in Pakistan-administered Kashmir. India paid back in the same coin with interest to Pakistan. The strikes destroyed Pakistan's militant-training infrastructures and killed many *jihadists* as per the Indian media. Pakistan denied the strikes took place. Their attempt to convert shame into honour was as futile an effort as that of an elephant trying to hide behind a pole.

Chittaranjan was not wrong when he had said that Pakistan would pay. But after the strikes, Pakistan was seething with rage and a feeling of revenge was paramount. They wanted to avenge the surgical strikes as they had eaten humble pie. India had made mincemeat of their ego. Pakistan was reeling under the humiliation of India's triumphant operations. To add to their humiliation, India's surgical strike team had returned safely with no casualties and that too after damaging Pakistani terror infrastructure, and killing many terrorists and their supporters on Pakistani soil.

With their policy of 'bleed India with a thousand cuts', Jaish-e-Mohammed was the chosen terror group for the next attack. With heavily armed and trained fidayeen fighters, their plan to target a very important army cantonment in India had been in place for months.

* * *

On 29 November 2016, General Qamar Bajwa took over as the Chief of Army Staff in Pakistan while Lt Gen. D.S. Hooda, who had led the surgical strikes as the Northern Army Commander in India, was retiring on 30 November 2016. Of course, Pakistan didn't want him to retire peacefully, so the attack on 29 November 2016 was symbolic in many ways.

Chapter 11

Merchants of Death

29 November 2016
4.30 a.m.–5.30 a.m.

It was around 4.30 in the morning on 29 November 2016, when Maj. Ajay woke up. He was the duty officer that week, and had to report to the headquarters (HQ) early in the morning. The HQ was about ten minutes away from the makeshift accommodation he was staying in. He left without waking up his wife Meenu as she had slept late the previous night. Amayra, their eight-month-old daughter, had been cranky all through the night. Noiselessly, he put on his uniform. A driver in a Gypsy picked him up.

***

Khalid, Aadil and Numan, the three terrorists, had planned to enter the Nagrota cantonment premises at around the same time. They had been hiding in the dry nullah the whole night, waiting for the change of guard.

The time had been chosen shrewdly as soldiers are inevitably a trifle distracted during duty change. In order to enter the cantonment, the trio had to climb a wall behind Maj. Ajay's accommodation. They had been trained to cause maximum havoc and death in the cantonment. But on seeing the Gypsy arrive at Ajay's house, they were forced to delay their plan. The driver of the Gypsy called up Ajay to let him know that he had arrived. But Ajay cancelled the driver's call and left after a loving look at his wife and daughter sleeping peacefully. He then gently closed the door shut behind him without latching it. It was common practice for him to not latch the door as the cantonment was quite safe and they had never felt the need to do so. He left in the Gypsy and was in his office in ten minutes.

***

The terrorists threw a rope ladder over the other side of the wall after hooking it on to a huge tree with many widespread branches. They didn't need to make much effort to cross the wall. Seeing Ajay leave the house, they assumed that there was no one else at home. Presumably afraid of being spotted in the outdoor light that had been left on, the terrorists did not venture near the house.

***

With a rucksack containing ammunition and AK-47s, the terrorists headed towards the sentry gate. They had strategically chosen that complex as it had easy access from the rear that had dense vegetation around it. It was almost impossible for the guards to notice them in that kind of terrain—not even the guards deployed at a height on a *machan*. The terrorists fired towards Sandeep, the sentry at the main gate of that complex. Before going ahead with their ghastly plan, they wanted to neutralize the sentry first, the main stumbling block in their path. The radicals knew pretty well that the only men with weapons would be the guards and after killing them, heavy casualties could be caused in a short time.

* * *

Sandeep was the only sentry at the gate. Knowing that it was vital to inform others, he sprinted from his post as though Yama, the god of death, was after him. He knocked at the two guardrooms to awaken the soldiers and alert them without making much noise. He kept walking to find a place to hide in and inform the others to send a backup team.

* * *

The first guardroom had two doors. One opened towards the sentry gate and the other was on the opposite side, at the end of the room. It was like a dorm with two lines of five beds lying parallel to each other. Usually, the mess staff and some transit soldiers of the Rashtriya Rifles unit were present there. Next to it was the second guardroom with similar furnishing. Right opposite this guardroom was a generator room and in between them was a path that led to the servants' rooms of the house occupied by Lt Mukul,

Lt Himanshu and Capt. Deepak. As one walked a little ahead of the servants' rooms, there was a staircase that led to a corridor. On one side of the corridor was Maj. Vinod's flat and on the other side was an empty flat. Both the flats on the first floor had a veranda and a terrace with water tanks. Maj. Vinod's roof had an LMG post.

* * *

A junior commissioned officer (JCO) was walking back from the toilet to the first guardroom when he saw three men walking towards him. He rushed towards the room and tried to lock it from inside. Khalid kicked the door not knowing that it opened only from the outside. The JCO shouted and tried to wake up Tarsem who was sleeping on one of the beds. Tarsem's guard duty was over and he was sleeping in the guardroom. Khalid, the butcher, shot through the ply door. One bullet hit the JCO in the stomach and the other pierced his thigh. He fell on the ground allowing Khalid to get inside and fire at Tarsem. Tarsem got hit on the head and knee and fell between the two beds.

Cold-bloodedly, Aadil shot at Grenadier Raghavendra Singh and Lance Naik Kadam Sambhaji Yeshwantrao, killing them instantly in their sleep.

Meanwhile, the sentry, Sandeep, managed to get into the servants' quarters of Lt Himanshu and Capt. Deepak's house. He woke up a member of the mess staff sleeping there and they locked themselves in the toilet. The scenario was grisly and changing every moment.

* * *

Numan, the third terrorist, hid himself like a snake in the generator room. He was expecting the Indian soldiers to retaliate in a big way against the havoc they had wrought on that tranquil cantonment. He was the only one with a silencer-fitted AK and the reason for that came to light only much later. Just then, Rifleman Asin Rai came out from the second guardroom with his AK. Numan was waiting for that moment. He took a clear shot at Asin and killed him on the spot. As Numan had emptied his AK, he took the magazine from Asin's rifle and fixed it into his, though the trio had carried plenty of ammunition to last them for a long time. Next, they walked up the path leading to the servants' quarters of Lt Himanshu and Capt. Deepak where Sandeep, the guard on duty was hiding with another soldier in the toilet. The mess staff, Virender, Inderjeet and Gurlabh, were holed up in the servants' quarters of Lt Mukul's flat.

***

Maj. Ajay's wife Meenu, who was woken up suddenly by the sound the gunfire, took some time to get her bearings. Amayra, their daughter, was sleeping peacefully next to her when she heard another sound, louder this time, of a grenade blast followed by firing. Could she be dreaming or was it for real? The only person she thought could confirm her fears was Ajay, so she picked up her phone and called him.

'Ajay, I'm hearing firing sounds near our place. They are very loud—I'm afraid it's some kind of an attack.'

While talking to Ajay, she was still rubbing her eyes to wake herself up.

'It's most probably firing practice nearby, Meenu. Don't worry. Just go to sleep.'

Ajay was aware how stressful it could be for a lactating mother with erratic sleep and hormonal imbalances. He was sure until then that it was sleep deprivation playing tricks on her. Meenu believed her husband even though her senses were telling her otherwise and hung up.

* * *

The JCO was alive and so was Tarsem who had been targeted in the first guardroom. A few minutes after the terrorists left the room, Tarsem called the HQ to inform them about the attack. It was Tarsem's call that had alerted the HQ and in turn, Maj. Ajay, who had just left the cantonment about fifteen minutes ago.

As Meenu pulled the blanket over her, ready to go back to sleep, she was surprised to find Ajay calling back. 'Meenu, there has been an attack on the cantonment. I need you to pick up Amayra and get down on the floor now.' Ajay was calm as usual. But being his partner, Meenu could sense the agitation in his voice. It is uncanny the way that women know so much about their husbands and Meenu was no different.

'And don't hang up. Just ignore any other call. Stay with me. Okay?' Ajay wanted his wife's assurance.

'Okay.' Meenu's response was short but fearful.

She took Amayra in her arms, spread a sheet on the floor and sat down with her. The firing got louder and more intense. The strongest survival instincts kick in when a mother has to protect her child from danger.

'Latch the door.' Ajay instructed Meenu as he remembered leaving the door unlatched in the morning, not wanting to disturb Meenu's sleep.

She hurriedly got up from the floor to lock the door from inside.

'I've locked the door,' she assured Ajay after sitting down on the floor again.

'Okay! Now position yourself and Amayra between the bed and the steel almirah and ensure you have cover from all sides.'

Ajay's instructions came from experience. He knew that the bed, almirah and the wall would give cover to his family from all sides. If a bullet were to be fired, it would be from at least a height of four to five feet so he asked them to lie down on the floor.

* * *

Shalini was also awakened by the sound of gunshots. On regaining her composure, she heard the gunshots closer. Unlike on previous occasions, she could not blame her pregnancy as the shots sounded far more real than the sounds of the hissing cobra she had heard before.

More so, her army experience had taught her to recognize that it was not the usual firing training.

Could it be a terrorist attack?

She had to be sure before calling anyone for help. When she heard a bigger blast, her experience was again at work to tell her that *it was a grenade blast.*

She hurriedly went outside to have a look. She saw flashes of lights behind her building that confirmed her doubts.

She immediately picked up the phone and dialled her adjutant. Without mincing any words, she said, 'Major, there is a terrorist attack underway. What should I do?'

Shalini was hoping that the adjutant would take her seriously and not think she was hallucinating because of the pregnancy.

'It must be firing practice going on, ma'am,' replied the adjutant who just was not ready to believe Shalini. People take time to believe the unusual.

'No! No! It's not firing practice. I can hear the gunshots right outside my house!' And then there was another blast that the adjutant heard over the phone as well.

After convincing the adjutant, Shalini looked around her house to determine from where the terrorists could enter. Her wooden front door was swollen and couldn't be bolted. She knew that it was going to be very easy for them to break in. Another way they could enter was through the air-conditioner vent that was open. There wasn't enough furniture in Shalini's flat to block these pathways. So, the first thing she did was switch off her flat's lights. It assured her that no one could see her from outside and made her feel a little less unsafe.

* * *

Maj. Vinod was fast asleep when the commotion began. His wife Bhanupriya and their one-year-old daughter Shreyasi were sleeping with him. He too was suddenly woken up by the grenade blast. The first one was a muffled sound, but the second was loud and clear—a grenade blast. Maj. Vinod immediately called up his unit 2IC, Lt Col Raina.

'Sir, we're under attack. You have to send in the QRT,' Vinod said shortly.

Bhanupriya, who had no knowledge about the army before getting married, was clueless and shaken. It was a dangerous situation to be in and she was glad her husband was there to protect them.

Ravi, who was receiving calls from everywhere about the attack, was worried. His commanding officer, Col Salvekar, was on leave and Lt Col Ravi was officiating as the CO.

It took him less than a few minutes to realize that the situation was grave. He started to get ready by changing into his combat uniform while his wife Anju kept receiving calls on his behalf.

'Ma'am, please inform sir that it is a terrorist attack,' Mukul requested Anju.

Mukul was staying alone diagonally opposite Vinod on the ground floor. His ankle had been fractured during a basketball game he had played a few days ago. He had already made a call to the battery commander, Subedar Randhir Singh, before calling his officiating CO. He knew that the team from the unit would reach them before any of the officers would.

Capt. Deepak and Lt Himanshu learnt through an SMS from Mukul that he had informed Ravi and the QRT was on its way. Ravi also received a call from Nandi about the attack and assured him of a QRT.

* * *

Within a few minutes, the QRT vehicle was at the complex gate but the firing from the terrorists was so heavy that it couldn't enter, leave alone attempt the rescue of trapped families.

Meanwhile, Maj. Kunal had a bulletproof *patka*[*] at his house as he was the duty officer. He got ready quickly with Uma helping him secure the bulletproof jacket and drove out in his car. When one choses initiative, one choses courage and Kunal was swift, like he had been during many other operations. Col Salvekar and Lt Col Ravi were counting on him. He was the most experienced officer in their unit when it came to counterinsurgency. He was also very intuitive and aggressive, yet calm and patient.

Kunal reached his unit in no time and got his gun issued.

'What's the situation, Randhir saab?'

Lt Col Ravi had changed into his combats and had asked his unit officers to meet him at his house so that they could all group up and address the site of the attack. Ravi was still busy answering his phone.

'Sir, the QRT can't get in. We need a bulletproof vehicle. It will be suicidal with the existing one. We are told that the fire is very heavy. Should we still get in?' Randhir inquired.

By then, Randhir and Lakhwinder along with their team had evacuated the JCO and Tarsem. They were taken to the Medical Inspection (MI) room for first aid and Lakhwinder stayed back.

'Who has a bulletproof vehicle?' Ravi inquired.

'51 Engineers, saab. They were on duty last night.'

---

[*] Bulletproof patkas are headgear designed to protect the forehead and sides of the head from bullets. They are used by the Indian Army, paramilitary forces and various state police departments. They can be made from a variety of materials, including hardened iron-steel alloy, Kevlar and nylon.

'Okay!' Ravi hung up and called the 51 Engineers commanding officer, Col Prakash, requesting him to send his QRT in a bulletproof vehicle.

* * *

Maj. Akshay Girish had woken up by then. He was in the bathroom to get ready for PT when he and his wife Sangeeta, heard the gunshots and grenade blasts. He opened the bathroom door and went out of the room to check what was going on.

'Sir, stay inside,' the guard outside their accommodation pleaded.

'Why? What happened?' Akshay asked.

'Sir, we aren't sure. There was an artillery drill planned in the morning but that was supposed to be at six. The firing started much before that.'

'This is not a drill, Sangeeta,' he told his wife.

'Then?' Sangeeta asked worriedly.

Without answering his wife, Akshay opened his cupboard to pull out his combat uniform instead of PT dress and started getting ready. He knew that time was of prime importance in situations like that. Bingo, their attention-seeking cocker spaniel, was strangely quiet as he watched Akshay put on his boots.

Sangeeta was trying to cover her three-year-old daughter Naina's ears with pillows so that the sounds of the firing didn't wake up her. Nothing is more worrisome for a mother than a cranky child who has woken up before they should.

* * *

In the meantime, Akshay's commanding officer, Col Prakash, called him saying that a QRT in a bulletproof vehicle was being readied. As he exited the door, Akshay turned around once to look at Sangeeta and said, 'You must write about this.'

Sangeeta watched him stride off, hoping that he would turn back to wave, but he didn't look back even once. As he disappeared, she could feel her heart pounding. Though she took it as a response to a life-threatening situation, the heavens above were sending her a signal that she willingly ignored. Sangeeta then went back inside to Naina and Bingo.

* * *

Akshay rushed to his regiment and got to know that a very young officer was on duty that day. That young officer was new to the station and wasn't even aware of the army complex where the attack was taking place. He then told Col Prakash, 'Sir, let me go.' Col Prakash agreed immediately, relieved that Akshay would be in charge.

When one has the will to serve others, he always ends up doing good work. Memories of stopping terrorist infiltrations in Kupwara flashed through his mind, and intent on helping his men and saving families stuck in the complex, Akshay moved out.

* * *

Col Prakash called up Ravi to inform him that the QRT had left with Akshay as its commander. Ravi asked Col Prakash to let Akshay know that he should stay in touch with Kunal who had already reached the unit. Their unit was about 500 metres from the complex where the attack was underway.

Ravi was in the midst of dealing with constant calls when he decided that it was imperative for him to be at the location. He was not able to wait any longer so he decided to move out in his personal car. Waiting for an official vehicle would have only wasted more time and time was of the essence to officers like Lt Col Ravi. The entire cantonment was sealed. There was an inner cordon by the army and outer cordon by the J&K police and Central Reserve Police Force (CRPF). Ravi was met with some resistance by CRPF vehicles at the gate due to the sealing of the cantonment but he wasn't ready to listen to any commands and protocols. He threatened the guard that he'd break the barrier if he didn't let him go.

'My men are inside. I need to get them out. *Do you understand?*' Ravi shouted.

He was desperate for no other reason than concern for his people who were stuck in the complex. He wanted everyone safely out. Trusting his instinct, the guard broke protocol and let Ravi out but said, 'Sir, you're in a civilian vehicle with combat uniform on. Anyone can mistake you for a terrorist. Be careful.'

Lt Col Ravi thanked him and sped to his unit.

* * *

5.30 a.m.–6.30 a.m.

Meanwhile, Maj. Akshay picked up Maj. Kunal who was walking towards the complex and both the men entered the complex with the QRT. The mine-resistant Casspir vehicle immediately came under heavy fire from the terrorists with bullets pounding metal and glass windows, shattering the driver's rear-view mirror. It was pitch dark and only flashes of firepower could be seen. Akshay and Kunal waited for a while, but the firing didn't stop. So they asked the driver to drive on and park the Casspir away from direct fire. They got out of the vehicle and took charge of their area of responsibility as discussed. The darkness helped them deploy the team faster than usual.

* * *

Shalini by then was calculating how best to save herself. With very little furniture available at her temporary residence, she couldn't block the door and windows. She looked for all the possible options but when she couldn't find any solution, she decided to wait for someone to come and rescue her. Different people have different defence mechanisms for survival and often instinct kicks in. If one has to keep waiting in such a situation, it feels no less than a lifetime of imprisonment. She kept looking out of the window to be better informed about the situation outside. In such a situation, the process of seeking god is accelerated manifold. Shalini chanted the *Hanuman Chalisa*. She knew that she couldn't change destiny and remembering god was only going to give her the strength to face the situation.

Maj. Vinod was now concerned as the firing had become heavy and he could hear the gunshots almost outside his house. Like everyone else in the cantonment, Vinod hadn't latched the door of his house either. He hurriedly went to the door to latch it. He then placed iron and wooden trunks in front of the door along with the dining table.

He couldn't latch the outer door because if he did, he would have been exposed in the gallery that connected the two doors. The gallery stretched into a veranda and Vinod hear some kind of constant movement there. He wasn't sure who it was, but he was not willing to take a chance. He then took Bhanupriya and his daughter Shreyasi into a bathroom that had no windows and was in the centre of the house. He was almost sure that no bullet would reach them there. But the firing was getting more intense as the QRT was firing back from where the terrorist onslaught was coming, which was his veranda. Vinod looked at his phone that had very low battery. The transformers were blown and there was no electricity in the complex.

'Where is your phone?' Vinod asked Bhanupriya, who was trembling with fear.

'It's in the room,' she quivered.

Vinod squatted and moved into his bedroom and got Bhanupriya's phone so he could get in touch with his people outside. To protect Shreyasi as best as he could, he took a mattress lying nearby and rolled it around her instructing his wife, 'Just make sure she doesn't cry.'

He then made a few calls to check on Capt. Deepak and Lt Himanshu.

* * *

Himanshu and Deepak had done the same with their doors—barricaded them with whatever heavy objects they could lay their hands on.

Deepak got his voluminous medical books and tied them around himself and Himanshu.

'What are you doing, sir?' Himanshu asked.

'Making ourselves bulletproof,' Deepak said, while tying more books with the help of a rope.

'Will they work?' Himanshu was puzzled while looking at his padded waist.

'Why don't you go out and try it?' Deepak said sarcastically and returned his attention to dealing with the life-threatening situation they had landed into out of the blue. While handing over a pair of dumbbells to Himanshu, he instructed, 'It's a do-or-die situation. Take hold of these firmly and hit them hard on the face if someone enters this room.'

'Yes, sir.' Himanshu, fully aware of the impending disaster, nodded.

* * *

Uma, Maj. Kunal's wife, was worried sick and wasn't sure if she should call Kunal. But after a while she gave in to the worry and called up her husband, who immediately picked up the phone.

'Are you okay?' she inquired.

'Yes, I'm fine and the operation is underway. Don't worry. I'll keep you informed.' Knowing that Uma had a disposition to worry, Kunal always kept her informed of all that was happening around him.

'Please take care of yourself,' Uma said as calmly as she could. She didn't want to appear frantic and distract her husband from discharging his duties.

* * *

Havildar Sukhraj, who was responsible for the post with the LMG on top of Maj. Vinod's house, saw Aadil and Khalid climb up the staircase. Though the LMG placed on the roof wasn't easily visible from below due to its height and branches of trees nearby almost brushing the roof, Sukhraj was worried. He knew how much more dangerous the terrorists would be if they took that position so he rushed from the mess across to the staircase leading to Vinod's house. Aadil saw him approaching but didn't take a shot at him. He let him come closer. And Sukhraj who had nothing else on his mind but getting to his gun position as soon as possible, didn't see Aadil as he hurriedly climbed up. When Sukhraj came near, Aadil shot him in the head. He fell and rolled down the stairs and lay dead at the bottom. True to the nation, true to his duty, Havildar Sukhraj was the fourth soldier the terrorists killed.

If Sukhraj wanted, he could have turned his back on his duty and saved his own life. It was an easy and obvious choice that many in his place would have made. If he did that, he would have certainly been questioned, reprimanded or even court-martialled, but he would have been alive today. Is there anything more important for a person than being alive?

Life is all about the choices we make. As long as Sukhraj lived, he didn't let himself down on this account. And when he died, he didn't leave a chance for anyone to question him.

His choice: 'Nation First' was inscribed with those bullets in his body.

He died a hero.

Chapter 12

When Bullets Reigned Supreme

6.30 a.m.–7.30 a.m.

Army bigwig Lt Gen. A.K. Sharma, who was the corps commander, 16 Corps, was woken up by a phone call telling him about the attack on the fringes of Nagrota Station. He took some time to realize which unit it was. He knew that infantry soldiers were very sought after and were on the Line of Control. They were not available in the station to counter that attack. He understood the units that were available were engineer regiments or regiments of artillery, which had a different functionality. They were neither trained nor equipped to handle such an attack. He then decided that they had to call in the para to minimize the damage—they already had four casualties.

The challenges faced by the Indian Army were manifold. First, they had to pin down the terrorists to the area they had entered as there was an ammunition dump close to the complex boundary. Apart from that, there were about 300 families residing barely 500 metres away. In case the fidayeens escaped from the complex to that area, they could cause massive death and destruction. Another challenge that Gen. A.K. faced was to keep the media at bay. From his experience, he knew what had happened during Kargil, the Mumbai terror attacks and at Pathankot. He didn't want the operational details to go out into the public domain through the media as they were dealing with a sensitive, terrorist-initiated, hostage-like situation. Any relay of that on television would have given live updates to the operators across the border. He made sure that the media didn't enter the operation site.

The army was also apprehending a hostage-like situation as the terrorists were right outside the houses of the officers. It had to make sure that none of the officers or their families were taken hostage because negotiations to secure the release of the hostages seriously harm national interests and often turn ugly.

Hindsight offers rosy alternatives, but ground reality paints an ugly picture.

If only Indian Airlines flight IC814 hadn't been hijacked, the hijackers would not have asked for the release of Masood Azhar. Jaish-e-Mohammed would have never been formed nor would the attack on Nagrota have taken place.

or

If only Omar Abdullah had not propagated the rehabilitation policy for terrorists, Munir would not have come to India and aided the fidayeens who attacked the Nagrota cantonment.

* * *

Chapter 13

Massive Losses

Maj. Sumeer was the alert troop commander of the contingency response team when his para unit received a call regarding the attack.

'I'll take the alert troop and move immediately, sir.' Maj. Sumeer was calm while responding to his commanding officer. He had just finished the routine physical training and quickly changed into his combat uniform, donning a maroon patka and DMS (direct moulded sole) boots. DMS boots are ankle boots with a moulded plastic sole that were introduced by the British Army in 1958. The boots were similar in appearance to the ammunition boots used during World War II. He then got into a Gypsy with a few men and the *dhai* (two and a half) ton vehicle followed them. It was a team of about thirty people with the best training and experience, and they were carrying sophisticated weapons. By then, the CRPF, J&K Police and the army had cordoned off the area.

***

'Now just relax and don't panic. Our team is trying to clear the area,' Maj. Ajay assured Meenu. Being at the headquarters, he was aware that para was on its way.

Getting up from the floor to see what was going on outside, Meenu exclaimed, 'It's quite dark outside. I can only see flashes of light.'

On partially drawing the curtain to see what was happening outside, she was quite relieved to see men in Indian Army uniforms. That gave her the confidence to fully draw the curtain. And just when she did, a bullet went through the window, narrowly missing Meenu. It hit the wall opposite. Meenu ducked in an instant. Ajay could gauge from Meenu's heavy breathing that something wasn't right.

'What happened?' he asked.

'I think I just dodged a bullet!' Meenu blurted out and rushed to grab her daughter. It was at that precise moment when Meenu realized the situation outside was more than life-threatening.

'*What are you doing, Meenu?*' Ajay screamed angrily.

'I was just trying to find out what was happening outside,' Meenu said with bated breath.

'Don't do that. Listen to me. Just lie down calmly on the floor with Amayra. I'll come soon and take you out,' Ajay assured her as calmly as he could.

He knew the seriousness of the situation but didn't want Meenu to go into a state of panic. But even during that tense situation which caused emotional turmoil, Meenu hadn't lost her pragmatic side. She knew that the latch would not hold the door for long if someone wanted to forcefully enter and take them hostage. She looked around and zeroed in on a chair, a few boxes and the fridge. She dragged all of that to block the door by placing everything against it.

* * *

Maj. Kunal and Maj. Akshay along with their team were engaged in a long stand-off with the terrorists.

'How many do you think are there, Akshay?' Maj. Kunal asked over a call.

'Sir, I feel there are at least three on the building facing your mess. Most of the firing is coming from that area.'

By then no one was sure of the number of insurgents inside the area. Also, Aadil and Khalid were changing positions quickly, and randomly firing to create an impression of there being more men involved. Their plan was to divert the attention of the forces towards them to allow Numan to move around freely and cause maximum damage.

'Okay, I'll try to get Shalini and Nandi out. You pin those bastards there.' But as Kunal tried to climb the stairs to get Shalini, there was an under barrel grenade launcher (UBGL) blast. This shocked the officers as they were now realizing the insurgents' wide range of ammunition. The UBGL is a grenade-launching weapon attached to a rifle and can be very destructive. Kunal stopped and called Akshay, 'Can you send someone with me to give me cover?'

Akshay asked Subedar Jung Bahadur of his unit to accompany Kunal in the evacuation process. Jung Bahadur took a position on Shalini's terrace, giving Kunal cover to conduct his recce.

* * *

Kunal knew who was exactly at what position as he was acquainted with that area while Akshay was new to that location. Akshay's responsibility was to not let any terrorist escape from that complex and enter the other populous complex, while Kunal's responsibility was to evacuate the officers and families from the residential buildings. Naik Chittaranjan Debbarma, a sharpshooter, was asked to take a position on the lawn. Facing Vinod's building with an LMG, he hoped to get a clear shot at Khalid or Aadil.

***

By then, Ravi had arrived with his QRT in a CRPF bulletproof bunker vehicle. He was waylaid by Lakhwinder at the gate, who had been informed of the situation and briefed Ravi accordingly. Ravi was also in constant touch with his unit officers. The firing from Vinod's building was very heavy as both Khalid and Aadil had taken positions on the veranda of that building. Aadil was right outside Vinod's house. Making an assessment of the situation, Ravi decided to first evacuate Nandi as there was no firing from that block.

***

When the firing stopped for a while, Shalini drew the curtains to see what was happening. She couldn't see much but could hear a vehicle approaching her building. Now, there were two bulletproof vehicles standing on the road leading to her building. One was facing Vinod's building and the other was facing the road with its back towards Shalini's building. That vehicle had Lt Col Ravi and his QRT with Naik Lakhwinder. The firing had stopped because Aadil, Khalid and Numan had put their weapons down to offer namaz. That opened the window of opportunity for Maj. Kunal and he went upstairs to evacuate Shalini. While Khalid and Aadil were in the respective verandas of Vinod's building, Numan with his AK with a silencer was on the move. When Khalid and Aadil moved up the building, Numan moved towards Shalini's building.

The fidayeens wanted destruction and the core of that feeling was the religious sentiment drilled in them by their handlers who wanted India's destruction. That gave them a sense of legitimacy in doing what they were doing.

* * *

'I'm getting a call from my brother.' Meenu put Ajay's call on hold and attended to her brother's call.

'I just heard the news. Is everything okay with you?' her brother asked, concerned.

'I'm fine and with Amayra in the house. Ajay is trying to get us out. Don't worry,' Meenu assured her brother. The reason for his worry was the news that everyone in the country was watching. It had horrifying details that Meenu was unaware of until then.

'Is the attack so serious that it's in the news?' Meenu questioned her brother who until then had gauged that Meenu was being kept in the dark intentionally. Ajay didn't want Meenu's brother to reveal too much to her so he called him and said, 'Don't tell her anything. She will panic.'

Ajay's brother-in-law understood and prayed that Ajay would get his sister and niece out of danger soon.

Ajay then resumed his call with Meenu as he didn't want her to be out of contact even for a moment.

* * *

Mukul could barely walk and he was the most vulnerable as his house had a big fragile glass window. He could hear Khalid move to and fro in the veranda, and from his window, he could also see the man's shadow. He called up Ravi and said, 'Sir, can you get a weapon dropped at my place? I know the exact location of one and can take a shot at him.'

But Ravi's experience told him to wait. Ravi knew that Mukul was injured and he didn't want to take any chances with the number of casualties rising. He just had one aim in mind and that was to evacuate everyone safely.

* * *

Himanshu called up Mukul and asked him about his well-being.

'I wish I had a weapon. What's the point of dying without even putting up a fair fight?' It was Mukul's regret.

'Of course, we will give them a fight, sir. We are all charged up with dumbbells in our hands and fat medical books around our waists. Let them enter my place once, and I'll make sure that they regret taking birth, let alone attacking our place.'

Mukul suppressed a laugh. They kept the conversation to minimum as they didn't want the terrorists to know of their helpless presence in the flats. Mukul switched on his iron as it was his only weapon against those extremists.

* * *

Ravi got the bunker vehicle parked below Shalini's flat and just outside Nandi's flat with its door open and waiting for her.

'Ma'am, please come out,' Kunal said, knocking at Shalini's door. Jung Bahadur was with him keeping vigil.

'Why should I come out? What's your identity?' Shalini was apprehensive.

'Ma'am, I'm Major Kunal. You need to come out quickly.' Kunal also gave the information about his unit. Shalini was convinced after that and stepped out of her flat. Kunal escorted her to the vehicle, and just when he was about to get into it, he spotted a shadow.

'I think I saw someone. Sir, you continue. I'll join you later,' he told Ravi.

'Get into the vehicle, Kunal!' Ravi almost held Kunal by his collar. Just then the hydraulic door of the vehicle started closing.

'Saab, don't go alone. I'll come with you!' Lakhwinder jumped out of the vehicle with its door half-closed and joined his favourite officer. Kunal had always stood by Lakhwinder like all the other men in his unit. They climbed up a pipe to the top. Lakhwinder remained on the terrace with Jung Bahadur but Kunal followed his instincts and came down the staircase. He was almost sure that a terrorist was hiding around that building. Just then the firing from Vinod's building started again with Aadil and Khalid screaming, '*Allah-Hu Akbar*'. They had finished namaz and started firing indiscriminately again. They didn't have specific targets except for Sukhraj who had fallen into their laps. Khalid and Aadil were more of a tactical distraction ploy while Numan aimed shots with his silencer-fitted AK.

Their strategy worked when Numan shot Kunal who was coming down the stairs. He got shot from the side, and the bullet punctured his liver and other vital organs. He tried to walk towards the vehicle but then he would have been exposed.

'*Saab ko goli lagi hai!*' shouted Lakhwinder. He was so loud that Vinod, Deepak and Himanshu heard him. Lakhwinder was about to jump ahead to hold his beloved saab when he realized that Kunal was exposed to the terrorists.

'Saab, please try to come around so that I can pick you up,' Lakhwinder pleaded.

Kunal dragged himself, holding his wound while Lakhwinder asked Jung Bahadur, 'Saab, please give me cover fire. Even if you have to empty the magazine, don't hesitate. I'll come back and give you another one. But for now, I have to save Kunal saab!'

Jung Bahadur did as he was told. He fired across the board. Lakhwinder jumped from the terrace and lifted Kunal up.

'Open the door, goddamnit, open the door!' Ravi was shouting.

Lakhwinder helped Kunal get into the vehicle. He sat beside him and removed his turban to tie it around Kunal's waist to stop the bleeding.

'Sir, I know that bastard's position! Take me back before he escapes. We can still get him.'

* * *

Ravi and Nandi asked Kunal not to speak after they saw blood coming out of his mouth. The bunker vehicle stopped at the gate and Nandi took him to the MI (medical inspection) room. The MI room didn't have the necessary equipment so he was transported to Jammu Military Hospital in an ambulance where he was declared dead on arrival. A mother had lost her son, a wife had lost her husband, a daughter had lost her father. But most importantly, India had lost one of its bravest and brightest officers. Kunal didn't put his own safety before the nation's in spite of Uma's request, because his duty was towards his country first, his men second and then his family and himself. He had done his best and that's all that mattered to him on the last day of his life.

7.30 a.m.–8.30 a.m.

It took less than an hour for Maj. Sumeer to reach the site of the attack, but a little more time to find his bearings in the commotion. The strategy, equipment and tactics used by the para are quite different. They undergo one of the most intense physical and mental trainings only to face situations like the one that lay in front of Maj. Sumeer at that moment. He took a briefing from the officers who were present there. Chief of Staff Maj. Gen. Gajendra was in a bulletproof vehicle along with his team and were firing at Vinod's building. Akshay and his team were still deep inside the place from where Shalini and Nandi were rescued. Maj. Sumeer took a brief of the situation from the chief of staff as he was in the middle of the fighting arena with his team and had fresh information.

* * *

It was around 7.45 a.m. when Chittaranjan called his wife, Namita Debbarma. In the midst of heavy firing, he felt a desperate need to let his loved ones know what he was engaged in at that moment. In a precarious time like that, a responsible man wants his family to be prepared for any eventuality. When he heard that Maj. Kunal was hit, he realized the possibility of him getting hit was high as he was more exposed on the lawn, firing at the terrorists than Maj. Kunal was. He took his mobile phone out of his pocket with his left hand while he kept firing with his right. He had Namita's number in the last dialled list of his mobile and he clicked on it to speak to her. The phone rang for a while without any answer from the other side. Namita would always take the mobile with her wherever she went, but that day she had gone to the fields to work without it. She never expected her husband to call her so early in the morning as he would usually call her up during the evenings when he would get some free time. So, Chittaranjan called up his sister, but she too didn't pick up the phone. Thereafter, he called up his brother-in-law. 'I'm in the middle of a terrorist attack and may not be able to call after this. There are bullets flying everywhere. Please inform my mother and ask her to pray for us. Only her prayers can save us now.'

He used the word 'us' because he knew that no matter who lived or who died, they were going to suffer, die or live together. That was the world of a soldier.

* * *

Meghna, Akshay's mother, was sick with worry after Akshay's wife Sangeeta informed her about the situation. She messaged on their family WhatsApp group that included Sangeeta, Meghna, Girish—Akshay's father, Neha—his twin sister and Pradish—Neha's husband, about the attack in which he was fighting bravely.

Meghna immediately called Sangeeta to know more.

'Ma, we have been asked to stay inside and not move out. There are two sentries outside the house.'

Listening to this, Meghna was deeply troubled but she hid her anxiety and motivated her daughter-in-law to have faith that everything would be all right.

'I can't talk much, ma, we have been asked to remain quiet.'

Meghna understood Sangeeta's predicament and disconnected the call only after telling her to be courageous. However, what she told Sangeeta didn't seem to work on herself. She immediately switched on the television to watch the news. By that time, the army had already lost Kunal. The news of Kunal's death was flashing all across television stations, adding to Meghna's anxiety. Her heart was pounding and little droplets of sweat were trickling down to her ears and cheeks. Her hands and feet were as cold as ice. She remained glued to the television when Pradish asked everyone to get off the family group, so that their anxiety was not read or felt by Akshay, and he could concentrate on the work at hand.

* * *

Thereafter, Meghna and Sangeeta—the two women out of three, who meant the world to Akshay—kept consoling each other, messaging constantly. Neha, on the other hand, kept her emotions to herself so that she didn't end up adding to the anxieties of her mother and sister-in-law.

* * *

Uma, Maj. Kunal's wife, along with the other regiment ladies, had gathered at Anju's residence. Anju was Lt Col Ravi's wife. Until then, she was not aware of Kunal's death though the other ladies knew. Anju didn't want to break the news to Uma yet. Since the others knew the situation, they couldn't hold their tears back and Uma kept wondering why they were crying until she received a call from her brother-in-law.

'How's Kunal?' he asked.

'He is fine. He is in the operation. I spoke to him around six,' Uma replied.

'No! He is not fine. How badly is he hurt?' he exclaimed.

Uma was confused and Anju took the phone from her. That made Uma dig further and she found a WhatsApp message floating around in the groups about Kunal's sacrifice. She still didn't believe it and switched on the television to watch the news. That cleared every doubt Uma had.

She ran towards the door to go out, but the other ladies held her back.

'Where are you going, Uma?' Anju questioned, holding her.

'I have to go and see Kunal!' she screamed, tears running down her face. She couldn't face the devastating reality of her world crumbling right before her. She collapsed and fell on the floor and was immediately taken to the hospital. Anju accompanied her.

***

The amount of ammunition that the three terrorists were carrying was enough to keep the army busy for more than three days. Mukul saw his unit team consisting of Maj. Sandeep and Chief of Staff Maj. Gen. Gajendra fire continuously at his building so that they could keep Khalid and Aadil pinned to the area.

Another person who was doing the same, possibly more bravely, was Chittaranjan, who was a part of Akshay's QRT. He held his ground on the lawns of the mess and kept firing continuously at Aadil and Khalid.

After a while, the terrorists fired at the bunker vehicle with a UBGL fitted on an AK. It was an armour-piercing grenade, but they didn't know that it required a priming range to have an impact. Thankfully, the grenade didn't burst. An immediate note of weaponry used by the terrorists was being made by the team on the ground.

***

Akshay was in the thick of the action. By then, he was aware that there was a third terrorist on the move who was causing the maximum damage. He wanted to take him on. Akshay and his buddy moved in a leapfrog manoeuvre around Shalini's block to flush out Numan, but he was hiding in the servants' quarters of that block.

Since it was darker inside than outside, Numan could take a clear shot at Akshay. He fired at him in close proximity. The bulletproof jacket worn by Akshay saved him from a few bullets but the impact flung him to the ground. Before he could recover, he had already been hit by two bullets. One pierced his shoulder and the other his waist below the end of the bulletproof jacket. He tried to crawl to take cover of the wall next to him but he couldn't get a grip. So he held on to the grass tightly in excruciating pain. Just then, Numan who had a clear view, fired a UBGL at him. Unfortunately, this time, the grenade burst after hitting Akshay's torso and he began bleeding from an arterial wound to his thigh.

* * *

Meghna and Sangeeta kept waiting for a message. Their anxiety kept increasing with time, even as Akshay's life was ebbing away. He had made the supreme sacrifice. He had given his life for the well-being of others. He didn't care if he was going to be remembered by his fellow countrymen or whether he was going to get accolades for his sacrifice. All that he cared about was the duty given to him and he performed that with diligence to the best of his ability.

He had looked straight into the eyes of death before meeting it like a valiant soldier. Akshay left behind a family he adored and countless memories.

* * *

Within a few minutes of Akshay sacrificing his life, Chittaranjan got hit by a bullet in the head. His mother's prayers were unanswered. When Namita returned from the fields, she tried her husband's number many times but by then, Chittaranjan's breath had left him. Had she taken the phone with her, she would have been able to hear her husband's last words and would have had something to cling on to for the rest of her life. But all she was left with was remorse.

Chapter 14

When the Siege Was Broken

8.30 a.m.–9.30 a.m.

It was during his second round of the area that Maj. Sumeer concluded that the major firing was coming from Vinod's block. He decided not to take any hasty decisions after seeing two dead bodies—Chittaranjan's in the nullah and Sukhraj's on the stairs of Maj. Vinod's block.

Naik Lakhwinder, who was in the team, was overwhelmed on seeing Chittaranjan and Sukhraj lying there and could only give vent to his grief lamenting, 'Saab, can we take them in?'

Sumeer asked him to hold on—he knew from their inert bodies that they were already dead. Getting them in at that point when all three terrorists were alive was nothing more than a suicide mission. And that certainly wasn't the kind of mission he was on. Sumeer's 2IC asked him to take a ladder and climb Shalini's building where Jung Bahadur was. But as he reached closer to the building, he saw the remaining members of Akshay's QRT sticking to a wall, taking cover. Sumeer had to switch tasks from climbing the wall to rescuing those men. Lakhwinder, who had promised Jung Bahadur that he would be back with a magazine, had brought it for him. At the time, however, it was important for the para to evacuate all those nearby and in the building, so that they could eliminate collateral damage and carry out their plans.

* * *

Sumeer reversed the vehicle with its door facing the building so that everybody could get in without wasting any time. Jung Bahadur was asked to jump from the terrace along with a few others. They doubted that Numan had a view of the stairs as Kunal had gotten hit while leaving the stairs and being exposed. Sumeer evacuated everyone from that building and brought them to a safe place.

On the way, Subedar Jung Bahadur told him, 'Saab, I think there is a terrorist in that building. Maj. Kunal was hit by him and I also believe that he has injured Maj. Akshay.' At that point, no one knew that Akshay had lost his life.

Sumeer called up his 2IC who cautioned him, 'Sir, I don't think it's a good idea to climb the building. There is a terrorist hiding there.'

By then, Sumeer had also realized that firing by Aadil and Khalid was only a decoy to divert the army's attention from the third terrorist. The army was concentrating on the building where Khalid and Aadil were, but it was Numan who was causing maximum casualties. He was hiding in Shalini's building.

* * *

The para team identified two hillocks facing Vinod's building and deputed two parties with rocket launchers on one hillock and a sniper on the other. The paras also took over the outer cordon from the already deputed party in order to have smoother communication and better operational control.

Sumeer then decided to concentrate on the visible enemy rather than the invisible one. The quadcopters and unmanned aerial vehicles (UAV), commonly known as drones, were giving them a clear view of Aadil who was on the roof of Vinod's flat. He wasn't firing then but just lying down on his stomach. Sumeer could see his position from his bulletproof vehicle as well. He informed the two hillock teams over the radio set to take a shot.

* * *

Maj. Vinod by then had removed the mattresses from his bed and wrapped Shreyasi and Bhanupriya in them. Khalid was taking cover of the pillar of the stairs of Vinod's building and firing. He was also raising slogans of '*Allah-hu Akbar*' and changing positions. Maj. Vinod heard a loud bang on his door and he immediately took out his mobile, the battery of which was almost dying and called up Ravi, 'Sir, someone's banging on my door. These guys may get inside!' Vinod was extremely worried for his wife and child.

Ajay could see what was going on around the complex of his house with the help of quadcopters equipped with cameras. They had taken position on a hillock and were firing UBGLs at the terrorist who had taken refuge on the terrace of Vinod's house. Ajay's house was somewhere in the centre of that hillock and Vinod's building, where two of the terrorists were positioned and firing.

* * *

Meenu kept feeding Amayra continuously to make her sleep. Meenu's milk did the job until around ten-thirty, but by then, Amayra had started to wake up and get cranky. Meenu was very worried. If the terrorists heard her baby cry, they would know of their presence.

'Ajay, Amayra has started to wake up. I'm giving her cough syrup.' At that time, it was the safest and only option that Meenu had, to make her kid go to sleep.

Due to the UBGL firing and its impact, the roof of Ajay's house was beginning to crumble. If the roof fell, his wife and daughter would be exposed. He asked the CO of the para to hold the firing. No matter how hard Ajay tried to calm Meenu, she had realized that it wasn't going to be easy for her and her daughter to escape alive. There were bullets flying in almost every direction around her house.

All that she wanted at that time was for her daughter to be safe and out of danger.

'Ajay, it's getting worse. Promise you'll get Amayra out of the mess. I'm not bothered about myself, but our daughter hasn't even started walking. She has her whole life ahead of her!'

Meenu burst into tears. Ajay felt quite helpless but also angry. The danger lurking outside his house was as real as his love for his wife and child. And he was ready to go through any hardship to get them out of it.

* * *

Ravi received information from Vinod about a terrorist banging on his door and passed it on to the para team. Sumeer knew by then that it would be next to impossible to get Khalid as he was smartly taking cover of the wall of the corridor. Without wasting any time, he told the rocket launcher (RL) para team on the hillock to fire. Moments after the firing, the banging on Vinod's door stopped. So did the firing by Khalid.

But Aadil began firing again. Sumeer had to strategize to get him. He got in touch with his CO, 2IC and the team on the two hillocks and decided on using a high-explosive (HE) air-bursting round.

'Sir, if we try motor bombing, the whole house will be blown away and we have families and officers stuck inside,' Sumeer informed his CO.

* * *

With the best of the skills anyone can have in the military, the para decided that they'd do an HE air-burst from the RL that would burst in mid-air, as per the range fixed on the nose of the round. Generally, every other fuse is impact-based. It bursts only after it has made an impact with the target but the HE, which is air-burst, is a special round that bursts in mid-air. It was a big risk, but less risky in comparison to motor bombing. The range was calculated from the hillock with the help of a laser range finder (LRF). The para team on the hillock repositioned themselves in order to get the right range to fire. After getting that range, they fired a few rounds of HE air-burst. The snipers from the other hillock were also taking shots at Aadil simultaneously. After a few minutes of firing, there was a lull. Sumeer and his team in the bulletproof vehicle had also exhausted their ammunition, so they went to the ammunition dump for replenishment.

After the reloading was done, Sumeer and his team headed to Shalini's block. The action was intense between Vinod's building and Shalini's building. Different teams were going inside in the bulletproof vehicles and reversing them at Shalini's block. When Sumeer's vehicle was being reversed, his weapon was pointing towards the building while the others had their weapons in other directions covering a 360-degree view. Numan was hiding in the servants' quarters of Shalini's building. When he saw the vehicle going back, he came out and started going up the stairs where he had shot Kunal. Sumeer spotted him and without hesitation, he started firing at Numan. Sumeer was sure there was no one from their side in that building because he and his team had evacuated them. He fired two to three double-tap rounds at Numan and hit him in the leg. He screamed in pain and fell down, and Sumeer and the team heard him. Numan tried to pull himself up but couldn't do so. From his torso downwards, he was exposed and Sumeer took that opportunity and fired an entire magazine into him. By then, Sumeer's men also started firing at Numan from the vehicle. Numan shakily picked up his AK and randomly fired at Sumeer's vehicle. One bullet hit very close to the opening from where Sumeer was firing. The buzzing sound of the bullet was so loud that Sumeer fell down. Meanwhile, Numan was injured waist-down and was completely immobile. He took a grenade from his pocket to hurl it at the vehicle. Just when he was about to swing his arm, Sumeer took aim and instantly killed him. The grenade remained in his hand as he lay dead. At that time there was only one war and that war for Sumeer was life against death. He had clearly won.

* * *

Karma comes back to you in one way or another. It could be today, tomorrow or years afterward, but it does happen, and usually when you least expect it; that too in an entirely different manifestation as divine retribution. For those three terrorists, karma was following them ever since they jumped over that wall. They died exactly the same way they had killed others. Kunal, Akshay, Chittaranjan and Sukhraj sacrificed their lives in action, protecting the lives of their countrymen and will forever be remembered as heroes. But no one will ever know the names of those three murderers except the government records in which they are termed as 'terrorists'.

* * *

Para stopped firing and planned an evacuation soon after Ajay apprised them of the situation. He drew a map of the complex since he knew the area well and the para team asked him to join them to evacuate Meenu and Amayra so that they could proceed with their operation.

'I'm coming to pick you up. Grab all the essentials and be ready. I'll knock at the door and call out your name; don't open the door until you hear my voice,' Ajay instructed her clearly.

Meenu, who was in shorts and a T-shirt, hurriedly changed into a pair of jeans, while lying down on the floor. She looked around for essentials that Ajay had asked her to carry. Her *mangalsutra* and her baby were the only essentials in that moment; nothing in life was more important to her than her loved ones.

After a few minutes, Ajay knocked at the door. He had come with a team of para soldiers. Meenu opened the door and was overwhelmed looking at her husband. She knew for sure that no force in the world could now do her or her daughter any harm when her husband was around.

After a fleeting hug, Ajay picked up Amayra.

'Ma'am, there is a vehicle parked outside. You have to take a big leap and get into it. It's higher than other vehicles.'

The CO waited for a few seconds to make sure Meenu had followed his instructions and continued, 'You have to think that this is a movie shoot and you have only one take. You're required to do everything perfectly in that one take. When you get into the vehicle, don't look back and do it as quickly as possible because we will follow you. Our safety also depends on how quickly you board the vehicle.'

Without wasting any time, Meenu took a big leap as instructed and got into the bulletproof vehicle. Ajay and the others followed her. Once they got into the vehicle, the CO asked them to smile for a picture he wished to click for the record.

'Ma'am, this is going to be your most treasured memory.' The CO tried to cheer up Meenu, who was sobbing profusely. He was glad that along with his team, he had been successful in evacuating the lady and her eight-month-old child out of an explosive and life-threatening situation.

Epilogue

The para continued their combing operations. They had to ensure that there were no more terrorists hiding anywhere in the cantonment. During the search, Sumeer found a dead body lying on the ground, its fingers clutching the grass tightly. When he bent down and turned the body over, Sumeer knew for certain that the person was one of his own men—the uniform and the weapon were identification enough. But he wasn't aware of the identity until he turned it over and saw the pocket tag: 'Major Akshay'. Sumeer stood frozen with grief, thinking how brave Akshay was to have plunged into the very thick of action and laid down his life for the cause he so passionately espoused. Willingness and initiative come much before abilities and sensibilities. Only when one feels that he is responsible for something, he becomes willing to take action. Akshay, who was in every way ever-willing and responsible, proved it by offering up his life. It was with an extremely heavy heart that Sumeer broke the terrible news of Akshay's death to the others. But he had no time to grieve over the death of his buddy—he was busy with the combing operations with his unit.

* * *

Anju, who was taking Uma to the hospital in Jammu, was distressed to see her friend distraught. She thought Uma didn't deserve to know about her dead husband, Kunal, via television news or from a WhatsApp message. When they reached the hospital, the doctors put Uma on medication. After a while, she got up and started talking to herself in Marathi, 'I've got very little time—I have to join Kunal before he leaves,' she mumbled.

Uma was hysterical and Anju tried to calm her down by reminding her of her daughter, Umang.

But Uma, overcome with grief, was in a different world and pleaded, 'I've told Kunal that my mother and his sister-in-law will take care of Umang. I need to be with him before he leaves. Please let me go,' Uma pleaded.

A helpless Anju kept requesting the doctors to take care of Uma. The doctors could only sedate her for a while, but Uma was drowning in a sea of pain at losing her husband— her whole world. She had lost her soulmate. Sedatives can calm the body but not a badly wounded soul.

Anju could stay in the hospital with Uma until half past ten that night. She had to get back to her little children and husband, Ravi, who also was in the thick of the combing operations and had no time to even mourn the loss of his comrades. Anju reached home and called Ravi—she longed for a fleeting glance of him to see that he was okay. Her heart wept for Uma because she knew that it could have been her husband and not Kunal. She hated to leave Uma alone but wasn't allowed to stay in the hospital at night. In the morning, Kunal's family reached Jammu and they were by Uma's side. She opened her eyes only at half past eight in the morning and found her sister-in-law beside her.

* * *

Sangeeta and the other women and children of Akshay's unit were shifted to MES IB, a kind of guest house that was away from the location of the attack. When she tried to ask the officer helping them in the shifting process about Akshay, he subtly ignored her queries saying, 'Ma'am, all is good. Please get into the vehicle. We have to shift you all to a safer place.'

Once in the safer location, the ladies sat on the lawn looking after their children. Meghna, Akshay's mother, kept trying to get in touch with Sangeeta, but by then, phone jammers were active and it was difficult for a call to get through. Sangeeta, after a while, called up Col Prakash, Akshay's CO, and asked, 'Col Prakash, I can't get in touch with Akshay.'

'Ma'am, Akshay is inside. We're in touch. Don't worry.'

But Sangeeta could make out from his fumbling tone that he was lying. She had a gut feeling that something wasn't right. She then tried to call other officers to get some information about Akshay but they all seemed to be ignoring her or digressing from her queries. In fact, none of them had the courage to tell her the truth. After a few minutes, Col Prakash came to see Sangeeta. The way he looked at her was enough for her to know that she had lost Akshay. She held Col Prakash by his collar and cried. Overwhelmed by the sudden turn of events, she screamed in pain, while her three-year-old daughter Naina stood looking at her. When she saw her daughter looking totally lost, she stopped screaming. She had to control herself for Naina's sake. To spare the children from being terrified by the tragedy, Sangeeta was taken to another room away from them.

* * *

Meanwhile, Col Prakash called up Meghna, who was anxiously waiting for some news about her son. Meghna took the call nervously, hoping for the best. But hearing Sangeeta wailing in the background, she knew the worst had happened. As Col Prakash broke the heart-wrenching news to Meghna, she nearly lost consciousness and fell heavily into a chair. She called up her husband Girish and after the initial disbelief, they grieved their brave son. Akshay's twin, Neha, refused to believe he was no more. She kept googling the news and saying, 'No, papa, there's nothing in the news. It's a mistake. It can't be Akshay. They've got it all wrong.'

She was clinging on to their last hope—there was no news about Akshay on TV. But that hope was short-lived, when Akshay's name was flashed on television and the news of his sacrifice was confirmed. The entire family was devastated and benumbed with shock. Pradish, Neha's husband, booked tickets for everyone to fly out the very same night to be with Sangeeta and Naina, and have a last glimpse of their valiant Akshay.

* * *

Sangeeta's request to see Akshay was denied as the post-mortem formalities were yet to be completed. Her grief at her husband's death was massive and unspeakable, and she was barely in her senses. To calm her down, she was about to be administered a sedative, but she refused to take it. Finally, when the doctors convinced her, she fell into a slumber, exhausted after the emotional turmoil she had gone through.

The next morning, Sangeeta was taken to a guest room near the military hospital in Jammu. Meghna, Girish, Neha, Pradish and her own parents joined her. No words were spoken. Meghna saw that her daughter-in-law had gone pale. She hugged Sangeeta tightly, giving her all the warmth and love she had. She then saw Naina who was sitting on the commode even after finishing her business. Meghna hugged her tightly before cleaning her up. All of them then went to the morgue in the military hospital where the bodies of Akshay, Kunal, Chittaranjan and the others who were killed in action were lying in state.

* * *

Sangeeta was handed over Akshay's beret, watch and mobile phone by a soldier. Though the beret was soaked in blood, his favourite G-Shock watch was spotless. Sangeeta brought his things close to her chest and burst into tears. She felt as if she was in Akshay's arms and he was smiling and whispering into her ears, 'I won't let you fall, my love.'

So true. Akshay did keep the promise he made to Sangeeta before starting their journey as partners. His sacrifice had, in fact, catapulted Sangeeta to the exalted pedestal of 'Shaheed ki Patni'.

* * *

Kunal's belongings—a watch, a ring, a silver bangle and his mobile phone—were handed over to Kunal's sister as Uma had still not come to terms with her husband's death. She remained under the impression that Kunal was only injured. Denial was a self-inflicted mechanism to keep her from facing the harsh truth.

* * *

Much later, Uma and Sangeeta were allowed to see their husbands after the post-mortem formalities were over. Some suggested that it wasn't advisable as they should be remembered as living and full of life, not dead. But Meghna refused to listen to anyone. She wanted to see her raja beta and went inside the morgue with Girish. Only two people were allowed at a time. A person on duty opened the ice compartment and Meghna saw her dead son who still had a smile on his face. She broke down and her screams echoed outside the morgue. She frantically touched her son's face and body. She tried to open every bit of plastic he was wrapped in to feel him. She cupped his face in her hands and ran her fingers through his hair. Girish tried to stop her but to no avail—her love for her child had suddenly changed into unbearable grief. She felt bereft. Girish tried to calm her, and after a while, she got back her composure and made way for Sangeeta and Neha to have a look at Akshay's body.

***

Uma, who did not believe that her husband was no more, kept trying to wake him up. She wasn't sure if all the good times spent with him were enough for her to carry on. She wanted more of him. But she was slowly coming to terms with the fact that Kunal was gone. When she intently looked at her husband's dead body, he seemed to have come alive before her, reminding her of his words before their marriage, *'I could come home wrapped in a tricolour.'*

For a moment she felt as if Kunal was with her and smiling, *'See, Uma, I was true to my words—I've come to you wrapped in a tricolour.'*

But where was Kunal? Everything had been consigned to the past by that elusive entity—time. Who doesn't wish to turn back time and relive the ecstatic moments in one's life? Uma, though a brave soldier's wife, was after all a human being.

***

All the seven bodies were flown to Delhi where they were given a twenty-one gun salute and then flown to their respective hometowns, and handed over to their families for the last rites.

***

A few days later, a staff member from the bank visited Chittaranjan's adjutant to let him know that Chittaranjan's loan was sanctioned and he could proceed on leave. The adjutant gave him a blank look. He didn't know what to say. He just took the papers from the bank staffer and thanked him. At the same time, he wondered, 'Did the man not see the news? Didn't he know that brave Chittaranjan had died protecting them all?'

It was nothing special that Chittaranjan had done as a soldier. Any soldier true to his commitment to the nation would have done the same. But the adjutant wanted the bank staffer to not only know but also remember the sacrifice his jawan had made for him, for Nagrota, for the nation and, most importantly, for humanity. As the bank staffer was about to leave the adjutant's office, he said, 'Chittaranjan died fighting the terrorists. He fought bravely until the last bullet in his rifle. And I want you to remember his sacrifice. Jai Hind!'

The bank staffer looked at the adjutant in disbelief. His words were enough to moisten his eyes. He saluted him saying, 'Jai Hind!' and left the office.

Akshay, Kunal and Chittaranjan, all three who showed indomitable courage during the attack on Nagrota, were not even supposed to be there on duty on 29 November 2016. Their presence on that terrible day can conveniently be blamed on destiny. But was it destiny that choose them or had they chosen their own destiny? Destiny is not always a matter of chance but sometimes a matter of choice. All the three had voluntarily and dutifully chosen to be there. They didn't care about their families nor about themselves. They didn't care whether they were going to get any accolades for their duty or sacrifice. They didn't care if they were going to be remembered by their countrymen for whom they had laid down their lives. All that they cared about was their duty and doing it with utmost dedication and pride. Their sacrifice and the courage of brave hearts like Sumeer and Sukhraj saved India from a potentially dangerous hostage-like situation. They saved a pregnant Shalini. They saved Meenu and her daughter Amayra. They also saved Mukul, Himanshu, Deepak, Vinod and his family and so many others.

* * *

It would be highly inappropriate on my part to say that they didn't save Meghna, Sangeeta, Uma or Namita. In fact, they helped transform their tears of sorrow into those of pride. It took Akshay, Kunal and Chittaranjan a while, but they did save the women they so passionately loved.

JUSTICE T.S. THAKUR
FORMER CHIEF JUSTICE OF INDIA

AFTERWORD

The annals of Indian military history are replete with stories of valour and sacrifice, but not all of them have been told or written about. Fewer still have been narrated in a style as gripping as Bhaavna does in her book, *Nagrota Under Siege.*

The dastardly attack on Nagrota by militants was bravely countered and overcome by Indian soldiers. We lost seven of our men in the operation. Narratives such as these honour their sacrifice, as well as the sacrifices that their families make.

The author's extensive research into this event underscores her deep commitment to accuracy and nuance. By presenting this account that fully and accurately captures the attack and the Indian Army's operation, Bhaavna enriches our collective memory and encourages dialogue on the implications of such experiences.

Extremely readable is this narrative that immortalises the sacrifices of the brave hearts who defended the garrison at Nagrota.

Justice T.S. Thakur

A-160, NEW FRIENDS COLONY, NEW DELHI - 110025
TEL: 011-49097550 | EMAIL: justicetsthakur.infodesk@gmail.com

In Conclusion

It has taken me five years to write this book and throughout the journey of writing it, which included visiting the site of the incident and conducting interviews, I've had mixed emotions of regret, loss and pride.

Regret, because I had to make the families of the soldiers go through the pain of reliving the traumatic events in which they had lost their dear ones. I have not only heard their stories but also listened to them. It would be wrong if I said that I feel their pain because what they have lost is unimaginable. But if listening to their stories could bring tears to my eyes every time I listened or wrote them down, I can't even begin to imagine what it must have been like for them. I personally apologize to each one of them for making them relive those moments of pain.

Loss, because every soldier who laid down his life in that attack was important not only as a father, husband, son or brother but also as an important soldier of the Indian Army. The loss of a soldier in many ways feels personal. And why should it not? They died protecting you and me.

Naina and Umang were barely three and five when they lost their fathers, Maj. Akshay and Maj. Kunal, respectively. Mothers do everything to protect their sons, but the brave end up finding a good reason to die. Their mothers would have desperately wished that they should have never cut the umbilical cords that connected their sons to them. If only they could have held their sons close, away from harm. Girish, Akshay's father, suffered a mild heart attack after a few weeks of losing his son. Uma went through years of counselling to help her move on and take care of Umang, who is her hope and purpose of life now.

Pride, because I believe that things don't happen accidentally. The universe conspires to lead you towards a purpose. I have been most privileged to have got the opportunity to write about these brave hearts. A story that would have been lost in the archives has been put forward for all of you to realize how big a sacrifice it takes to keep our country safe. It's an opportunity for you to acknowledge, cherish and remember the sacrifices made by our soldiers.

Meghna has never shied away from her responsibilities, and Sangeeta and Naina were the most important of them. Meghna waited for Sangeeta to heal so that she could ask her to get married again. And then after a few years, just as she had wished, a boy came into Sangeeta's life. Meghna nudged the relationship forward. She convinced Sangeeta to tie the knot and move on in life. Though Sangeeta's wounds haven't healed and will never completely heal, she has found new and beautiful reasons to once again fall in love with life. Though Naina remains her papa's daughter, she now has a father who is equally, if not more understanding and loving.

Meghna also runs a trust in her son's name. The Major Akshay Trust works to strengthen patriotism and service to the nation and stands in solidarity with and support of families of brave hearts and war-wounded soldiers. She believes that her raja beta wants her to be busy with good work and not mull over his absence.

Lt Gen. A.K. Sharma, the then corps commander, made sure that the Pakistan Army was unable to sleep on their side of the border for many months after the attack. The loss was personal to him, like it was for all soldiers. He is now retired and lives with his family in Panchkula.

Uma has found peace in spirituality. She loves to sing and recite the Gita. She spends her time looking after her daughter, Umang, being both a father and mother to her. And that is exactly what Maj. Kunal would have wanted her to do.

Namita, Chittaranjan's wife, was able to build a house for herself and her in-laws with her late husband's provident fund savings. She continues to take care of her ailing in-laws. Her children, Inlet and Kuplai, are in college and Class IX, respectively.

Meenu's daughter is now eight years old. Meenu was blessed with a son in 2021 who she lovingly named Arjun after the great warrior in the epic, the Mahabharata. She now lives with her children in Mohali as her husband Ajay is posted at a field station where families are not allowed.

Lakhwinder, who played a major part in the operation, retired in September 2018. He now lives in Rorki with his wife. His son, Armaanpreet Singh, is preparing for the JEE exams. Lakhwinder, along with his wife, looks after his small agricultural land in his village.

Maj. Vinod, Capt. Himanshu, Maj. Sandeep, Col Ravi, Lt Mukul and Maj. Deepak continue to serve in the army with honesty and sincerity.

SSP Hamid Ansari, DIG Rahmatulla Gurbaz and IG Ahmed Khan were all promoted, with one of them joining the Research and Analysis Wing (RAW).

Maj. Sumeer chose premature retirement and has joined the police services. He lives with his wife and two children.

Maj. Akshay, Maj. Kunal and Naik Chittaranjan, like many others, had volunteered to be a part of the Nagrota operation. Sometimes, when warfare is voluntary, one loses the best men first. In the middle of absolute insanity, they displayed extraordinary courage and sacrificed themselves. Their courage needs to be admired, remembered and emulated.

I will, and I hope you will too.

Acknowledgements

This book stands as a testament to the bravery, resilience and unyielding spirit of those who lived through the Nagrota attack, and it would not have come to life without the invaluable support of many extraordinary individuals.

My deepest gratitude goes to Timmy Uncle, my rock throughout this journey. His guidance and unwavering belief in this project propelled it forward, ensuring these words would see the light of day.

Gen. Hooda, Gen. Ved Malik, Gen. Ian Cardozo, Neeraj Kumar and Maj. Poonia—your meticulous reviews and seasoned insights have given this narrative a depth only a few could impart. Surinder Lal Sir, thank you for diving into those first edits with such care and dedication. Gen. Khandare, I thank you for the foreword; and thank you, Justice Thakur, for the afterword.

I would like to thank S.P. Vaid, former DGP, J&K, whose support helped me understand the story from an overall perspective. His experience with the J&K Police provided authenticity to the story.

Maj. Gaurav Arya, Gaurav Sawant and Shiv Aroor— thank you for taking the time to offer authentic and thoughtful reviews, lending this story a credibility that

187

only voices like yours could provide. My heartfelt thanks to the intelligence team in Nagrota for granting me access to the site and allowing me to immerse myself in the story's physical roots.

To the NIA, your unconditional support was a bedrock upon which this story was built. Maj. Sumeer, thank you for generously sharing your own story; your contribution enriched the narrative beyond words.

A special note of thanks to Col Pankaj and Col Tripathi for their steadfast support in ADGSC—your faith and efforts added layers of strength to this journey. Gen. Ajae Sharma, your willingness to be interviewed was the spark that planted the seed for this book, allowing it to grow into a compelling story of courage and resolve.

Dr Anand Ranganathan and Samar Khan, your insightful reviews have been an honour to include. And Anupam Kher, for lending your esteemed endorsement, thank you. Meghna Auntie, your constant support and guidance gave this book the finish it deserved— transforming it into a thrilling story that I hope will inspire generations to come.

Finally, to every brave soul who trusted me with their story, you are the heart of this book. Thank you for allowing me to carry forward a piece of your journey. This story would not be what it is without each of you, and I am endlessly grateful.

Scan QR code to access the
Penguin Random House India website